IFUT
A HISTORY

The
Irish Federation
of
University Teachers
1963-99

Marie Coleman

Published by
IFUT
Irish Federation of University Teachers
11 Merrion Square, Dublin 2, Ireland
Cónaidhm Éireannach na Múinteoirí Ollscoile

© Marie Coleman

January 2000

ISBN 0 9537151 0 8

History - Trade Unions - Ireland

Printed from camera-ready copy and bound by
Elo Press Ltd, Dublin, Ireland

Contents

Introduction and Acknowledgements	i
Abbreviations	iii

Part I - Organisation

What is IFUT?	1
Foundation of IFUT, 1963-1965	3
Development of IFUT's Internal Organisation, 1960s-1990s	6
Philosophy of IFUT	26

Part II - Activities

Industrial Relations	36
Response to Government Policy on Higher Education	58
International Activities	87

Conclusion   97

Appendices

1.	Chairmen and Presidents of IFUT, 1965-1999	99
2.	Secretaries of IFUT, 1965-	101
3.	Original Rules of IFUT	102

4. IFUT Member Institutions 106

Sources and Bibliography 107

The Author

Marie Coleman was born in Castlepollard, Co Westmeath in 1973. She graduated from University College Dublin with a BA in medieval and modern history in 1994, and a PhD in modern Irish history in 1998. She held the studentship in Irish history from the National Library of Ireland, 1998-99. Her book, *County Longford and the Irish Revolution, 1910-23*, will be published in 2000. She is married to Peter Martin and lives in Dublin.

Introduction and Acknowledgements

The aim of this work is to provide an outline of the main events in the history of the Irish Federation of University Teachers. In particular, an attempt has been made to highlight the importance of its dual role as both a professional association and a trade union by analysing its principal activities in the areas of education policy and industrial relations. As IFUT is still a relatively young body, the various stages in its organisational and structural development have also been examined. The importance of its international contacts, which sometimes appear to receive less recognition because of the predominance of issues such as salary negotiations, is also emphasised.

This is a study of IFUT based mainly on the activities of the central organisation; practicalities of time and space have not allowed for an in-depth study of the Academic Staff Associations, as the local branches of IFUT are also known, but there is ample scope for further development of the history of IFUT by focusing on the activities of its local branches. Similarly, the principal activities undertaken by the Federation are those which are focused on.

I am indebted to a number of people associated with IFUT for their assistance with this project: the President, Maureen Killeavy, and the General Secretary, Daltún Ó Ceallaigh, for detailed discussions on IFUT's activities and policies; and Phyllis Russell, the Office Supervisor, for facilitating use of IFUT's archives. My understanding of the workings of the organisation, and of the significance of a number of events in IFUT's history, was enhanced by interviews with active members, past and present; in this regard I wish to express my thanks to Jim Dooge, Enda McDonagh, Kieran Mulvey, Paddy O'Flynn and Val Rice.

Abbreviations

AIUT	Association of Intermediate and University Teachers
APSCE	Association of Professional Staffs in Colleges of Education
ASA	Academic Staff Association
ASTI	Association of Secondary Teachers, Ireland
ASTMS	Association of Scientific, Technical and Managerial Staff
AUT	Association of University Teachers
CSW	Commission on the Status of Women
DCU	Dublin City University
ETUCE	European Trade Union Committee for Education
HEA	Higher Education Authority
IAAM	Irish Anti-Apartheid Movement
IAUPL	International Association of University Professors and Lecturers
ICTU	Irish Congress of Trade Unions
ICUTO	International Conference of University Teacher Organisations
IFUT	Irish Federation of University Teachers
MSF	Manufacturing, Science, Finance
NUI	National University of Ireland
RCSI	Royal College of Surgeons in Ireland
SIPTU	Services Industrial Professional and Technical Union
TCD	Trinity College Dublin
TUI	Teachers' Union of Ireland

IFUT - A History

UCC	University College Cork
UCD	University College Dublin
UCDA	University College Dublin Archives Department
UCG	University College Galway
UL	University of Limerick
UTASA	University Teachers' Association of South Africa
WUI	Workers' Union of Ireland

Part I - Organisation

What is IFUT?

The Irish Federation of University Teachers is a professional association and a trade union which represents principally academic staff in universities and other third-level educational and research institutions in the Republic of Ireland. It has a membership more than 1,400 covering nineteen such institutions (these are listed in Appendix 4). Full membership is open to academic and professional staff in these institutions. There are also provisions allowing for membership in the following categories: honorary, associate, retired and postgraduate.[1]

The principal objects of the organisation are to advance higher education and research; promote and protect academic freedom; protect the terms and conditions of employment of its members; and safeguard their professional interests.[2] The chief activities undertaken by IFUT in pursuit of these objectives lie in the areas of industrial relations and state policy on higher education. IFUT is the body chiefly responsible for representing academic staff in salary negotiations. It is also the voice of university teachers in the media, and makes representations on behalf of university teachers to the government and the Higher Education Authority.

IFUT employs a full-time General Secretary, in effect the chief executive of the organisation, with responsibility

---

[1] *IFUT Rules*, June 1998: rule 3, pp. 2-3.
[2] *IFUT Rules*, rule 2, p. 1.

for administration, negotiation and research. With the exception of the General Secretary, all IFUT officers are elected from the membership. A President is elected each year at the Annual Delegate Conference and the maximum term so far served by a President is three years, although two years is more usual. The overall governing body of the Federation is its Council, which is responsible for formulating general policy subject to the supreme authority of the Annual Delegate Conference. The Council is composed of the incumbent and outgoing presidents along with delegates elected by the local branches of IFUT within each member institution. The policies drawn up by the ADC and the Council are implemented by the Federation's Executive, which also attends to the general business of the Federation. In the majority of the third level institutions affiliated to the Federation there is a local branch of the organisation, also known as the Academic Staff Association. Some of the smaller institutions, which have only a few IFUT members, form the Central Branch.

The Annual Delegate Conference provides an opportunity for the wider membership to have an input into IFUT policy and decisions. It also serves to inform members on the activities of the Federation during the previous year through the production of an Annual Report for the conference. The publication of a newsletter, *IFUT News*, and the maintenance of an internet web site also ensures that members are kept up to date on the workings of the Federation. These media are especially important for keeping members informed of the numerous and frequent changes in salary scales.

Foundation of IFUT, 1963-65

Prior to the formation of the Irish Federation of University Teachers, the only organisation which had ever represented teachers in higher education in Ireland was the short-lived Association of Intermediate and University Teachers (AIUT). Established in Cork in 1897, the AIUT aimed 'to embrace the assistant masters of the various Intermediate and University establishments in Ireland in an organisation of their mutual interests, and for the improvement of their position'.[3] This body was not limited to teachers in universities; it catered also for those who taught in intermediate schools. The introduction of the 1908 University Act altered the status of such schools, a move which, along with the formation of the Association of Secondary Teachers of Ireland (ASTI) in 1909, made the AIUT redundant. The AIUT was absorbed into the ASTI in July 1909.[4] While the ASTI catered for the teachers in intermediate and other secondary schools, university teachers were to remain without a representative body for more than fifty years.

The impetus for the formation of a body to represent university teachers was the establishment of the Commission on Higher Education, chaired by Cearbhall Ó Dálaigh, to

---

[3] Quoted in John Coolahan, *The ASTI and Post-Primary Education in Ireland,* 1909-1984 (Dublin: ASTI, 1984), p. 6.
[4] Ibid., pp. 13-14.

examine the reforms needed to cope with the projected increase in demand for places in Irish universities. The commission, which sat from 1960-67, represented the first initiative in higher education planning by an Irish government, and, as such, university teachers felt that their opinions should be presented to it. Moves which led to the formation of the Academic Staff Association in University College Dublin illustrate the views of academics in this regard:

> For some considerable time, and especially since the appointment of the Commission on Higher Education a number of members of the staff of University College, Dublin, have felt that consideration should be given to the formation of an Academic Staff Association in the College. The objects of such an association would be to improve the quality of university life in Ireland, to enhance the public reputation of university teachers and scholars, to further the interests of the academic staff and to represent them in all matters affecting their common interest...[5]

Along with such moves within individual universities, it was increasingly felt that there was a need for a similar association to represent the universities collectively. Thus, the idea of IFUT was born at a meeting held in the board room of University College Galway on 25 May 1963. It was attended by representatives from the five university institutions in the state: University College Galway, Trinity College Dublin, University College Dublin, University College Cork and St Patrick's College, Maynooth. The meeting agreed unani-

---

[5] Letter from T. Desmond Williams to all academic staff in UCD, 3 November 1960, UCD Archives Department, Robin Dudley Edwards Papers LA22/309.

mously 'that it was desirable to found an association of university teachers which would be independent of existing College Staff Associations'. The British Association of University Teachers (AUT), founded in 1919, was to be the model for this new body:

> It was agreed that the objects of the organisation would be the same as those of the British Association of University Teachers:
> "The objects of the Association shall be the advancement of University Education and Research and the promotion of common action among University Teachers and the safeguarding of the interests of the members". [AUT Rules, Article 2]

An interim committee was appointed for the purpose of drawing up Articles of Association for the new organisation.[6] Two years later, on 19 June 1965, the first Council meeting of the Irish Federation of University Teachers was held in Trinity College Dublin.[7]

The inaugural Annual General Meeting of the Federation was held in the Central Hotel, Dublin, on 26 March 1966, at which the principal business was the adoption of rules.[8] (The original rules, adopted in 1966, are reproduced in Appendix 3). It is interesting to note some of the changes which were made during the drafting of these rules. Initially it was suggested that the body would be called the Irish *Association* of University Teachers. However, the looser term of federation was eventually preferred. The rules as adopted opened

---

[6] Minutes of IFUT meeting, 25 May 1963, IFUT archives, file R8.23.
[7] IFUT file R8.23.
[8] IFUT file R8.6.

membership to 'all full-time and permanent staff of a University or University College or recognised College of a University in Ireland', whereas an earlier draft had proposed to limit membership to the Republic of Ireland. While this wording may have been preferred in the hope of attracting recruits from Northern Ireland such a situation has never materialised, and during the 1980s the rules reverted to the substance of the earlier draft for legal reasons; it was felt that IFUT could not cope with two different industrial relations frameworks and, therefore, should not leave itself open to a claim of entitlement to membership from somebody in a third-level institution in Northern Ireland. An early draft of the rules contained a provision that IFUT would constitute the Irish section of the International Association of University Professors and Lecturers (IAUPL); while this was dropped IFUT did affiliate to the IAUPL in the 1970s and withdrew during the 1980s in controversial circumstances which will be outlined in detail later.

Development of IFUT's Internal Organisation, 1960s -1990s

Growth of IFUT

During the early 1970s, as membership and the scope of its activities grew, the need for internal reorganisation within IFUT became apparent. A new member institution, the Royal College of Surgeons in Ireland, had joined. Government initiatives, such as the proposed merger of Trinity College Dublin and University College Dublin, and plans for the rationalisation of some faculties, along with the Federation's expanding role in salary negotiations, all of which activities will be discussed in detail later, led to a significant increase in the workload of officers.

From its foundation the administration of the Federation had been carried out on a voluntary basis by academics in their spare time. This system was no longer adequate to cope with the increasing volume of work. The first measure introduced to help alleviate the pressure on officers was the appointment of three members as Associate Secretaries in 1972.[9] This was added to the following year with the establishment of a Standing Committee, comprising the chairman of each staff association along with the officers of the Federation, 'to expedite the work of Council'.[10] Another innovation introduced in 1973 was the production of a newsletter which was circulated to all members to keep them informed of the latest developments in IFUT business.[11] Administrative difficulties were accompanied by financial ones; at the AGM in 1971, the Honorary Secretary warned that:

> The financing of IFUT itself is also a matter of some urgency. If IFUT is to continue to develop and play an active role in the many questions relating to Higher Education in Ireland then its finances will have to be substantially increased.[12]

This point, linked with the need for internal reorganisation, was reiterated at the following year's AGM:

---

[9] Annual Report, 1972, IFUT file R8.12.
[10] Annual Report, 1973, IFUT file R8.14.
[11] *IFUT News*, vol. i, no. 1, October 1973.
[12] Secretary's Report, 1971, IFUT file R8.11.

> ...if Council is to continue to take on all the work coming to it, if it is to communicate with members and to play a very essential role in University life of crucial importance to individual academics who otherwise may go unrepresented, or be heard only at local level, then a considerable reorganisation and very much greater financial backing will be necessary.[13]

Unionisation

One suggestion of how best to cope with the problems encountered by expansion was to transform the Federation into a trade union. An examination of the possibilities of unionisation began in 1971. The issue was discussed by Council at a meeting on 16 January 1971, having been raised by the Academic Staff Association in UCG. It was agreed that a subcommittee be established to examine the advisability of unionisation, the various means by which IFUT could become a trade union, and which of these methods was most suitable. The subcommittee consisted of one representative of each Academic Staff Association: J. McCarthy (UCD), Enda McDonagh (Maynooth) - who was also the convenor of the subcommittee - D. O'Donovan (UCC), Kader Asmal (TCD), D.B. Johnson (UCG) and R. Conroy (RCSI).[14]

An important factor in these moves to form a trade union was IFUT's increasing involvement in salary negotiations on behalf of academic staff in universities. In fact the need for a body to represent academics in matters relating to remuneration was one of the issues considered when the idea of form-

---

[13] Annual Report, 1972, IFUT file R8.12.
[14] Council minutes, 16 January 1971, IFUT file R8.28.

ing IFUT was discussed; at the meeting held in Galway in May 1963 'it was agreed that the organisation should have some form of negotiating licence for submitting salary claims'.[15] Within universities pressure was being put on the Academic Staff Associations to play a similar role; at the Annual General Meeting of the staff association in University College Dublin in 1968 the following motions were proposed:

> 1. The Academic Staff Association urges its Executive to concern itself with the salaries and conditions of staff members.
>
> 2. That the Executive Committee of the Academic Staff Association shall urgently seek to establish formal machinery for negotiation with College Authorities on the question of salaries.[16]

Prior to its examination of the unionisation proposal, IFUT had also begun to consider how it could formally establish itself as a salary negotiating body; Paddy O'Flynn, secretary of the UCD Academic Staff Association, reported on these moves to the Annual General Meeting of that body in 1970:

> Of more long term interest in the field of academic salaries is the current move by IFUT to prepare a scheme for salary negotiation which would develop formal machinery for negotiation on a national basis. This is still at an early stage.[17]

---

[15] Minutes of meeting, 25 May 1963, IFUT file R8.23.
[16] Minutes of UCD ASA AGM, 4 November 1968, UCDA, Edwards papers, LA 22/310.
[17] Secretary's Report to UCD ASA, 1969-70, UCDA, Edwards papers, LA 22/314.

The early activities of IFUT Council in this regard included writing to the governing bodies of all colleges in December 1968 to request payment of the 10th and 11th wage rounds as well as undertaking a survey of salary scales in Irish universities.[18] Pressure was beginning to be exerted from within for IFUT to formalise its role in regard to salary negotiation. This was highlighted by Patrick Masterson of UCD at a meeting of Council in November 1972:

> Professor Masterson drew attention to some of the present weaknesses of IFUT. He thought that many staff lacked confidence in IFUT being able to represent them on salary negotiations and were looking elsewhere. He believed that IFUT must show it had the political will to deal effectively with salary matters.[19]

Such a lack of confidence in the Federation's salary negotiating ability had led to a number of members in University College Galway leaving IFUT in preference for the Workers' Union of Ireland. The fear of losing more members in this way was also an important consideration in impelling IFUT to examine the possibility of becoming a trade union.[20]

At a meeting in March 1972 Council acknowledged the need for some change in the status of IFUT to enable it to represent its members in salary negotiations. It was agreed unanimously that the least which should be sought was Excepted Body Status.[21] This is the recognition accorded to rep-

---

[18] Annual Report, 1969, IFUT file R8.9.
[19] Council minutes, 11 November 1972, IFUT file R8.31.
[20] Interview with Enda McDonagh, 22 February 1999.
[21] Council minutes, 4 March 1972, IFUT file R8.31.

resentative organisations which are precluded from unionisation, such as the bodies which represent the Gardaí, in order to allow them to negotiate on behalf of their members. All of the colleges agreed to the need for a change in the status of the Federation, although opinion was divided on what form that change should take; Maynooth was in favour of affiliating to an existing trade union, UCD preferred to seek Excepted Body Status, while UCG favoured an examination of both options as well as that of forming a separate trade union.

The option of Excepted Body Status did not receive an enthusiastic response from the Department of Labour, which indicated that it would not grant such status to IFUT. It was felt in some quarters that the department's view was the result of pressure from the trade union movement which wanted to limit the number of organisations with excepted body status.[22] It had been agreed at the 1972 AGM that if Excepted Body Status was not granted unionisation would be proceeded with.[23] Thus, the formation of a trade union was made inevitable when on 7 September 1973, the Minister for Labour wrote to IFUT informing it that it would be inappropriate for him to confer Excepted Body Status on the Federation.[24]

Even before an investigation could begin on what form of unionisation should be sought, there was a considerable

---

[22] Council minutes, 8 April 1972, IFUT file R8.28.
[23] Annual General Meeting minutes, 1972, IFUT file R8.12.
[24] Details contained in a circular letter from John L'Estrange to IFUT members, 16 September 1973, IFUT file 8.52(I).

amount of debate among the membership on the advisability of the principle of unionisation. The case in favour stated that as the Higher Education Authority was pressing universities to organise formal salary negotiation schemes in any event, the formation of a trade union by academics prior to this move would ensure that a more desirable scheme could be achieved. Also, university authorities would be forced to take more notice of a trade union than a mere professional association, which would prove useful in areas such as expressing opinions about university promotions policies. Likewise, a trade union would be a more effective participant in decision making in regard to working conditions, teaching methods and research. It was also argued that a trade union would have a greater input into legislation relating to higher education. Aside from these views on the perceived greater effectiveness of a trade union over a purely professional association, those in favour of unionisation felt that a trade union would confer more cohesiveness and a stronger sense of identity on the academic community.

One of the main objections to unionisation arose from the implications of strike action, with many feeling that academics did not have a moral right to strike. There was also a fear that academic freedom might come under threat, in the form of discrimination against academics who did not join the union, and that in this regard discord and divisions would also be created. It was also argued that IFUT's role would be curtailed considerably, leading it to focus almost exclusively on salaries and related issues, to the detriment of educational ones.[25]

The subcommittee investigating unionisation examined all of the possible options. The chief drawbacks in seeking to form a trade union were the expense and the waiting time involved before a negotiating licence would be granted: a deposit of £5,000 had to be lodged in the High Court, and a membership level in excess of 500 had to be maintained for at least eighteen months, before an application for a negotiating licence could be made. As such IFUT could not become a fully fledged trade union until 1975 at the earliest. The formation of a trade union would involve the provision of a substantial range of services for the membership, including the establishment of a central office and the employment of an executive officer and secretarial staff. It was feared that because of its relatively small membership (approximately 600 in 1974), IFUT would have to increase its subscription if it could not improve the rate of recruitment. Based on these considerations, the subcommittee recommended that full unionisation could only be considered if a large proportion of the existing membership of the Federation joined the new union.[26]

The subcommittee proceeded to examine three forms of unionisation open to IFUT. The first, affiliation to an existing trade union, had been explored and discussed at length with existing unions, none of which seemed to welcome the

---

[25] 'Draft Subcommittee Report on Unionisation', n/d, IFUT file 8.52(I).
[26] 'Report on Unionisation', February 1973, IFUT file 8.52(I).

prospect of such a relationship. While this option would allow members to obtain services which were not then provided by IFUT, and the Federation would be allowed to retain its autonomy and identity, the subcommittee felt that the advantages were more apparent than real; the services obtained would be minimal, IFUT would still have to fund its own office and staff, and legal difficulties could arise in relation to immunities under the Trade Disputes Act and the Trade Union Act. As such, the subcommittee did not consider the option of affiliation to an existing trade union to be entirely satisfactory.

The second option investigated by the subcommittee was that of members of IFUT joining a trade union individually. However, this was not considered at great length as it was felt that it could lead to much internal fragmentation. The final option, and the one which was recommended by the subcommittee, was that IFUT should become a branch of an existing trade union. It was envisaged that IFUT would be constituted as a separate branch of a union, thus enabling it to retain as much autonomy as possible. This form of unionisation had the advantage of allowing participation in the Irish Congress of Trade Unions. In recommending this as the method of unionisation which IFUT should seek, the subcommittee took into account that many of its members were already in the Workers' Union of Ireland.[27]

This recommendation from the subcommittee was not greeted favourably by the Council of IFUT, which felt that

---

[27] Ibid.

the report 'did not give adequate reasons for the conclusions reached'.[28] Instead of acting on the conclusions of the sub-committee, Council decided to hold a ballot of the membership on the principle of unionisation and the preferred form which it should take. This resulted in an overwhelming endorsement of the principle of transforming the organisation into a trade union; to the question: 'Are you in favour of some form of unionisation as the most effective means in the present circumstances of establishing a national negotiating body for Irish University Teachers?', 475 voted yes, with only 143 against. The outcome of the ballot was less decisive in regard to the form which unionisation should take: the idea of forming an independent trade union received 227 first preference votes, while that of becoming a national branch of an existing union received 244. However, a majority of those who voted declared that they would become founder members of a unionised IFUT in both cases. While IFUT was now committed to becoming a trade union, further debate and consultation was required before a decision could be made as to the form which unionisation would take.

Council continued to maintain contact with the Worker's Union of Ireland and the Vocational Teachers' Association (the precursor of the Teachers Union of Ireland), to investigate issues such as the degree of autonomy which IFUT could maintain, the services which would be made available to members and the arrangements which could be made for members unwilling to join a trade union, in the event of it

---

[28] Council minutes, 17 February 1973, IFUT file R8.31.

becoming a branch of either of these unions. The means by which IFUT could become an effective independent union were also examined.[29]

The case for affiliation to the Workers' Union of Ireland (WUI) was set out by Art Cosgrove of UCD, who argued that, on its own, IFUT would simply be too small to be effective, whereas the WUI was a much stronger organisation. The benefit to be had from access to the negotiation machinery of the WUI was especially stressed by him. The opposition, arguing in favour of independent union status, was led by Cosgrove's UCD colleague, Paddy O'Flynn. In regard to conciliation and arbitration, O'Flynn argued, IFUT would be better represented by its own permanent General Secretary, than by a part-time branch secretary of the WUI. He claimed further that IFUT would have a larger membership as an independent union and that it would have a more direct role in the work of the Irish Congress of Trade Unions. O'Flynn rejected the view that the time scale involved before IFUT would gain its negotiating licence was as big of an obstacle in practice as it seemed in theory:

> We are at present awaiting the implementation of the 14th National Wage Agreement. This agreement will be operative from June '73 and will run through until the end of 1974. The possibility of a subsequent National Wage Agreement is at present rather doubtful but by that time the 18 months wait would be completed and a negotiation licence would be held by IFUT.[30]

---

[29] Council minutes, 12 May 1973, IFUT file R8.31.
[30] IFUT file 8.52(I).

Following some months of such consultations, Council finally made its decision on the form of unionisation which it considered to be the most appropriate for IFUT; the formation of an independent union was preferred. The principal consideration in arriving at this decision appears to have been maintaining the independence of IFUT:

> In Council's judgement the proposed arrangements with the WUI made insufficient allowance for the distinctive character and wide range of functions of IFUT, and involved certain restraints and departures from present practice.[31]

In particular, Council was concerned that the role of the Academic Staff Associations would be reduced and was dissatisfied with the requirement that the approval of the General Secretary of the WUI was needed before any statements or reports could be published.[32] Another important consideration influencing Council's decision was financial; it was calculated that it would be cheaper for IFUT to act as an independent union, as the general fund of the WUI would take most of the membership subscriptions if it became a branch of that union.[33] The vote of Council members in favour of the independent union option was decisive; 23 voted in favour, to 3 for the WUI proposal.[34] However, before unionisation could be proceeded with, the decision of Council had to be ratified by the members of the Federation. In a ballot held

---

[31] IFUT memo on unionisation, 22 October 1973, IFUT file 8.52(I).
[32] Ibid.
[33] IFUT file 8.52(I).
[34] IFUT file R8.31.

in November 1973, Council's action was endorsed comprehensively; 478 voted for IFUT to 'seek recognition as a Trade Union rather than become a branch of the Workers' Union of Ireland', while only 129 voted against.[35] IFUT's transition to a trade union was completed when it was issued with its negotiating licence on 30 January 1976.[36] As part of its trade unionisation IFUT established a central office and employed an Executive (later renamed General) Secretary to administer the Federation. Kieran Mulvey was appointed to this position in 1975.[37]

Following the transition to trade union status it was inevitable that the question of affiliation to the Irish Congress of Trade Unions (ICTU) would arise. The issue was raised by Kader Asmal in his presidential address to the 1975 Annual General Meeting:

> He outlined the serious developments now taking place regarding curtailment of wage claims and felt that there were many lessons to be learnt from the experience of the Association of University Teachers both in regard to salary negotiations and

---

[35] Results of ASA ballots on unionisation, November 1973, IFUT file 8.52(I).

[36] *IFUT News*, vol. ii, no. 6 (March 1977).

[37] Kieran Mulvey graduated from UCD with a BA in English and History. Before taking up the post of IFUT General Secretary he served as Deputy President of both the UCD Students' Representative Council (the forerunner of the Students' Union) and the Union of Students in Ireland. He remained with IFUT until 1980, when he joined the Association of Secondary Teachers in Ireland as Assistant General Secretary and later as General Secretary. He currently holds the position of Chief Executive of the Labour Relations Commission.

the balloting now taking place within the Association on affiliation to the British Trade Union Congress.[38]

He reiterated this point at an IFUT delegate conference in 1976 and at a meeting of Council in December 1977.[39] Eventually Council agreed to hold a ballot on affiliation to Congress, recommending that the membership vote in favour of the proposal.[40] As in the case of the decision to become a trade union, there was a debate among the membership on the merits and demerits of joining the ICTU. In favour of the proposal, it was argued that affiliation to the ICTU was a logical progression for IFUT, now that it had become a trade union. Other advantages cited were:

> the opportunity of participation in the work of a body which, increasingly, is accepted as the only proper voice of employees in Ireland...[the] practical advantage of research and information services available from ICTU to its members...Membership of Congress by IFUT might also be expected to promote a more harmonious development of unionisation among university staff.[41]

Opposition to the idea centred chiefly on the extent to which IFUT would be committed to supporting industrial action by other ICTU unions; Congress's 'all-out strike' policy was especially controversial. Fears were also expressed 'that IFUT is moving too far from its origins as a professional association into the mainstream of trade union organisa-

---

[38] President's address, 1975, IFUT file R8.17.
[39] *IFUT News*, vol. ii, no. 5 (July 1976), p. 5; Council minutes, 17 December 1977, IFUT file R8.41.
[40] *IFUT News*, vol. ii, no. 8 (October 1978), p. 2.
[41] Ibid., p. 3.

tion'.⁴² Such fears were clearly not seen to be of great import by the majority of IFUT members who voted in the ballot on ICTU affiliation, which was held in 1979; 84% voted in favour of joining.

IFUT came to play an active role in the ICTU. In 1980 its new General Secretary, Daltún Ó Ceallaigh [43] (appointed in 1980 to replace Kieran Mulvey), took up a seat on Congress's Public Affairs Committee, and has been part of a team, deriving from that committee, which conducts negotiations with the government on public sector pay. He also initiated and served as Secretary of a Council of Education Unions based on teacher unions which were affiliated to the ICTU, which was active during the 1980s and early 1990s.⁴⁴ The branches of IFUT are also active within the ICTU, through involvement in Congress's local Trade Councils. In a move which prefigured government legislation, IFUT secured the adoption of a motion calling for the decriminalisa-

---

[42] Ibid., pp. 3-5.

[43] Daltún Ó Ceallaigh was born in Belfast and studied at Trinity College Dublin, from where he graduated with a BA in History, Economics and Russian. Prior to his appointment as General Secretary of IFUT, he worked for the Irish Transport and General Workers' Union as Special Projects Officer and EEC adviser (1972-5), and then as Head of Information with special responsibility for international affairs (1975-80). He was also Director of the ICTU's Tax Reform Campaign (1979-80).

[44] The Council of Education Unions produced one volume of a journal, entitled *Aspects of Educational Development*, in November 1984.

tion of male homosexuality at the ICTU's Annual Delegate Conference in 1982.[45]

The status of IFUT as an independent trade union was debated briefly once more towards the end of the 1980s, when the possibility of a confederation with the Teachers' Union of Ireland was discussed. The initiative appears to have come from the TUI.[46] The question was discussed at the 1990 Annual Delegate Conference but the response was 'that there seemed to be no interest in this at any level of IFUT'.[47] However, a liaison committee between both unions was established and functioned for a time.

Structural Reform

Unionisation led to an increase in the membership of IFUT; the figures for 1974 were over 600, which had risen to approximately 900 by 1976.[48] However, there is some distortion in these figures, as they included some paper members; the actual paid-up membership was much smaller. Following unionisation the scope of recruitment was extended outside the confines of university academics, to include the staff in Colleges of Education and research institutes, and other categories of staff such as librarians, administrators, computer programmers and chief technicians (the latter in TCD

---

[45] Irish Congress of Trade Unions, *Twenty-Fourth Annual Report*, 1982, p. 211.
[46] IFUT Annual Report 1989, pp. 30-31.
[47] IFUT Annual Report 1990, p. 12.
[48] Secretary's Report, 1974 AGM, IFUT file R8.16; Secretary's Report, 1976, IFUT file R8.18.

only). The object of such expansion was to strengthen the fledgling trade union by augmenting its size.[49] A significant boost to membership was the affiliation of the Association of Professional Staffs in Colleges of Education (APSCE) to the Federation in 1980. This organisation, which represented teaching staff in St. Patrick's College, Drumcondra, Our Lady of Mercy College, Carysfort, Mary Immaculate College, Limerick and the Church of Ireland College of Education in Rathmines, was later to form the APSCE division of IFUT.[50]

This growth in the size of IFUT necessitated the development of more effective means of communicating with the Federation's members. The publication of *IFUT News*, referred to earlier, was the first step in this. This was followed by an experimental delegate conference, held on 20 April and 1 May 1976 in the Royal Marine Hotel, Dún Laoghaire. Attended by eighty delegates, the event was widely considered to have been very successful; according to *IFUT News*, it was 'The most important...event in the recent history of the Federation'.[51] The conference addressed a number of issues which arose from the Federation's newly acquired trade union status:

> a number of speakers indicated that it was essential that IFUT establish the kind of structure which would evolve a more dynamic role in terms of educational and trade union affairs.

---

[49] Interview with Kieran Mulvey, former General Secretary of IFUT, 10 February 1999.
[50] Secretary's Report, 1980, IFUT file R8.22.
[51] *IFUT News*, vol. ii, no. 5 (July 1976), p. 1.

Most speakers felt that the Federation needed to develop better relations with the media and to adopt a more determined position with the colleges vis-a-vis salaries, structures, transfers and pensions. It was also felt that a more regular communication with the membership was necessary so that they were aware of IFUT policy on a broad range of issues.[52]

The 1976 delegate conference was considered more effective than the system of AGMs which had been in operation since the foundation of IFUT in the mid-1960s. However, this new format was not continued. It was not until 1983, upon the recommendation of the General Secretary, Daltún Ó Ceallaigh, that an Annual Delegate Conference was instituted to replace the AGM.[53] In conjunction with this change, Ó Ceallaigh also instituted the practice of producing a full and formal annual report in advance of the conference to be debated at it by the delegates.

The replacement of the AGM was an example of how the structures put in place when IFUT was founded were no longer effective for an organisation which had grown considerably in both size and scope of activities during the first decade of its existence. The inadequacies of these structures were becoming obvious in other areas, in particular with regard to the composition and duties of the Executive and the Council. A discussion document was circulated in October 1976 outlining the need for changes in the way IFUT was governed.[54] It was felt that no clear division of labour had

---

[52] Ibid., p. 5.
[53] Ibid., vol. vii (Summer 1984), p. 12.
[54] 'Structure of IFUT for the Future', October 1976, IFUT file R8.18.

developed between the Council and the Executive, largely due to the fact that the Executive had not created a distinctive role for itself: 'its work has consisted mainly in preparing for meetings of Council. This results in a wasteful duplication of the work required of the most active members of the Federation'. Because of this the workload of Council had become excessive, leading to delays in policy-making, which should have been Council's primary function.

A smaller and reconstituted Executive of only seven members was finally implemented in 1981, at the suggestion of Daltún Ó Ceallaigh. In particular, Ó Ceallaigh had argued against all branches having representation on both the Executive and the Council, on the grounds that the Executive's functions were primarily managerial and an unnecessarily large membership hampered its efficiency. The post of Honorary Secretary was also later dispensed with, as it was no longer necessary in view of the development of the office of the General Secretary. This new format improved the administration of the Federation significantly:

> The year 1980-81 was the first one of the restructured Executive and the new arrangement has achieved its purpose of eliminating repetitiveness and sluggishness in conducting the business of IFUT. Instead, there is now a clear delineation between policy formation and execution, with a consequent speeding up and increase in the volume of matters dealt with.[55]

In fact, over time the Executive did acquire something of a policy role, but more by way of initial scrutiny of some items and making recommendations to Council to assist it in

---

[55] IFUT Annual Report 1981, p. 4.

digesting certain issues. Thus, a clear demarcation between the duties of the Executive and the Council has been maintained. There are only two instances when the Executive can exceed this demarcation. Firstly, when a need arises, between meetings of the Council, to react quickly on policy issues and an interpretation is assumed within the framework of existing ADC and Council positions. Secondly, when a similar situation to the first arises, but there are only limited positions to be referred to, and the best guess is made in the hope of retrospective endorsement. Neither of these situations occurs frequently.

One further adjustment was made to the new governing format in 1984 when, at the suggestion of the General Secretary, the quorum for Council meetings was reduced to 15 to rectify problems caused by poor attendance at Council meetings.[56] In spite of this, attendance at Council meetings usually rates at about only 30 out of 50. However, this can be explained by a *de facto* rotational approach to participation among Council members.

Among the other structural changes introduced by Daltún Ó Ceallaigh were the appointment of Convenors for Sections within Branches and the establishment of Groups. This is somewhat similar to a system of shop stewards. A Section can take industrial action, while a Group is purely for the purposes of liaison. The only strike by a Section within IFUT was that by librarians in UCD in 1980.

---

[56] IFUT Annual Report 1986, p. 4.

Another structural innovation introduced by Ó Ceallaigh during the 1980s was the creation of the Division, established for the purpose of grouping together Branches which possess a similar character and have distinctive interests. Divisions can form their own executives and hold separate AGMs. The only Division so far created has been the APSCE Division, composed of the Colleges of Education. However, APSCE has now been discontinued in the form of a Division, largely due to the reduction in the size of its membership following the closure of Carysfort, and is now simply a Standing Committee of IFUT. Nevertheless, the provision for the formation of Divisions remains, and may be employed in the future development or expansion of IFUT.

Philosophy of IFUT

Aside from its role in protecting the academic and material interests of its members, the Irish Federation of University Teachers seeks to promote and defend third level education, recognising the importance of both the teaching and research functions of a university. In his presidential address to the Annual General Meeting in 1974, Enda McDonagh highlighted the need for IFUT not to lose sight of its broader educational and social role; as it prepared to become a trade union, he feared that such considerations might become overshadowed by financial and material ones.[57] MacDonagh's successor as President, Kader Asmal, undertook a

---

[57] President's address, 1974, IFUT R8. 16.

campaign the following year 'to explain the role of universities in Ireland today'. The motivation for this campaign was two-fold; on the one hand it was a response to inadequate funding of universities by the government, and it also sought to counter allegations that universities were a waste of money by highlighting the necessity of universities in society for the provision of professional training and more general education.[58] The thinking behind such action was explained by Paddy O'Flynn in his presidential address in 1978:

> At times we may seem unduly defensive. This arises because our values come under attack from the various points of the political spectrum as being irrelevant. Our defensive role is accentuated by the failure of others in our academic community to articulate the value of university education to society as a whole.[59]

The best espousal of IFUT's philosophy of education is to be found in a document drawn up by the Federation, entitled *The Place of Higher Education in Modern Society*. Originally formulated in June 1984 as a response to the Fine Gael-Labour coalition government's *Programme for Action in Education, 1984 to '87*, it was later endorsed in a modified form by the Higher Education Working Group of the European Trade Union Committee for Education (ETUCE).[60] Rejecting the traditional view of the functions of a university

---

[58] Press statement on IFUT's campaign to explain the role of universities in Ireland today, 2 April 1975, IFUT file11.16(I).
[59] President's address, 1978, IFUT file R8.19.
[60] *IFUT News*, vol. xviii (Summer 1994), p. 1.

- 'the acquisition of knowledge by research and the transmission of knowledge by teaching' - as too narrow a perspective, it defined the relationship of the university to society:

> An adequate model must take account of its role in preserving and transmitting the cultural heritage of the society in which it exists; it must recognise its role in basic research, applied research and development, undergraduate general education, the education of professionals in such areas as medicine, pharmacy, engineering or teaching, adult education and in-service training, and the provision of professional and scientific consultants.[61]

The central function of higher education was deemed to be 'the advancement and communication of learning in all fields'.[62] This latter point highlights IFUT's insistence that research in the humanities is equally important as in the sciences.[63]

One of the principal targets for criticism in *Higher Education in Modern Society* was the increasing tendency to judge university performance on its economic cost-effectiveness:

> There is an ideology at large in which humanity's chief end is economic growth which rates cost-effectiveness as the supreme virtue. If this ideology is not resisted it will destroy not only our higher education institutions, but all our cultural institutions as well. Economic growth is good if, and only if, it is harnessed to improvement of the quality of life of the whole

---

[61] *The Education Action Programme - IFUT Response*, 1984, p. 3.
[62] 'The Place of Higher Education in Modern Society', in *IFUT News*, vol. xviii (Summer 1994), p. 1.
[63] *The EAP - IFUT Response*, p. 11.

nation. While higher education institutions must be publicly accountable, they must be judged not only on how they contribute to economic growth, but also on how they fulfil all their functions and contribute to the improvement of the quality of life.[64]

While not opposed to research being undertaken for commercial reasons, the Federation expressed its concern that commercial factors could come to dictate the direction of learning.[65]

University autonomy, defined as 'the necessary discretion of the university to manage its own affairs and set its own academic goals', and academic freedom, 'the term used to describe the intellectual liberty which is essential to academic staff if they are to perform their role as independent scholars, teachers and researchers', are two of the most vital aspects of the philosophy of the Irish Federation of University Teachers in regard to third level education.[66] The federation's response to the *Education Action Programme* highlighted the growing trend during the 1980s for governments to seek to exert greater control over universities, in many cases in order to achieve the economies referred to above, under the guise of making universities more accountable to the public:

---

[64] 'The Place of Higher Education in Modern Society', in *IFUT News*, vol. xviii (Summer 1994), p. 2.
[65] Ibid., p. 1.
[66] These definitions of university autonomy and academic freedom are taken from *The Universities Bill 1996 - Proposals for Amendment*, p. 1, a policy document prepared by IFUT in response to the universities bill.

> IFUT sees the growing public interest in universities as a healthy development and welcomes it; we have nothing to hide from the guardians of the public purse. But 'Public Accountability' must not be confused with 'Direct State Control'; IFUT welcomes the former but staunchly resists the latter...[67]

The numerous government proposals, and the great changes which have taken place in Irish higher education during the 1990s have brought a stronger restatement of its philosophy of education from IFUT. Opposition was voiced to what was termed as the 'enterprise culture' which was leading to an increasing trend of 'demand-driven' courses.[68] The need to preserve university autonomy and the principal of collegiality, in face of government attempts to exert more control over universities and to strengthen the executive role of university presidents, was stressed heavily in the addresses of IFUT Presidents to the ADC during the 1990s.[69]

A concept which has become commonplace to delegates attending IFUT annual conferences during the 1990s is 'massification', a word invented by the Organisation for European Co-operation and Development (OECD) to describe the substantial and sustained rise in the numbers of students seeking places at third level institutions. IFUT's greatest fear of 'massification' is that the expansion in student numbers will not be accompanied by a corresponding increase in funding to provide the resources necessary to

---

[67] *The EAP - IFUT Response*, p. 11.
[68] IFUT Annual Report 1992, president's address by Caroline Hussey, p. 20.
[69] IFUT Annual Report 1993, president's address by Anne Clune, pp. 20-21.

cope with the demands of educating much larger numbers of students. The situation was explained by the President of University College Cork, Michael Mortell, in 1994:

> State funds to the university sector are simply not nearly enough to match the projected student numbers. The Government does not seem to be responding to this obvious need, and I do not know if they realise the seriousness of the problem.[70]

In her presidential address to the Annual Delegate Conference of IFUT in 1994, Anne Clune posed the question which most concerned university teachers about this trend: 'How can quality of teaching be consistent with vastly increased numbers?'[71] She also voiced the fears of academics as to what the most likely scenario to deal with massification will be: 'It is very likely that this is to be the shape of things to come, that the adaptation of the existing system will be expected to take place without significant additional resources'. IFUT's policy that increasing student numbers must be accompanied by an attendant rise in funding was reiterated at the 1995 Annual Delegate Conference by the President, Eugene Wall:

> The Government must recognise that if they intend to increase the number of students in higher education, this will inevitably and unavoidably entail significantly increased expenditure on higher education. If the Government is unwilling to countenance this, they should grasp the nettle and limit the numbers entering higher education accordingly.[72]

---

[70] IFUT Annual Report 1994, quoted in president's address by Anne Clune, p. 24.
[71] Ibid., p. 24.
[72] IFUT Annual Report 1995, president's address by Eugene Wall,

Another emphatic statement of what constitutes the philosophy of the Irish Federation of University Teachers is to be found in the preamble to its response to the Green Paper on Education produced by Education Minister, Niamh Bhreathnach, in 1993:

> Since its inception, IFUT has consistently maintained a commitment to what it sees as the first principles in third-level education. These would include the human worth of the individual student, the dignity of university and college teaching, the importance of pure research, the international dimension to learning. IFUT contends that authentic scholarship and unwavering devotion to truth in all the arts and sciences constitute the essential foundations for teaching and learning and represent, too, the best service that third-level education can offer to society as a whole.[73]

The commitment to academic freedom was reiterated - 'academic freedom is an absolute prerequisite for the meaningful public service that a university institution by its nature is called upon to give' - as was the need for increased public funding in order to protect the quality of third level education. Greater equality of access to education was also stressed: '[IFUT] believes that third-level education should be readily available to all those students who would benefit from it, irrespective of social or class distinction'.[74]

Also in 1993, the Federation's President, Anne Clune, made a presentation to the National Education Convention,

---

p. 28.
[73] 'Response of IFUT to Green Paper on Education', in *IFUT News*, vol. xiv (Spring 1993), p. 7.
[74] Ibid.

which outlined many of the points raised in IFUT's response to the Green Paper. She emphasised the Federation's opposition to the application of the system of unit-cost funding to universities, which fails to measure the overall performance and contribution of a university, stressed the indelible link between the teaching and research roles of a university, and defended the collegial structure of university governance.

Another aspect of the Federation's philosophy which was raised in this presentation was its commitment to gender equality in university employment: IFUT sought improvement in the number of women holding senior posts in universities, and highlighted the need for the provision of crèche facilities, parental leave, job-sharing and career breaks. In order to ensure such improvements the Federation proposed the appointment of an equality officer in each university.[75]

A commitment to gender equality in the academic community has always been an important issue for IFUT. In 1972 the Federation made representations to the governors of University College Cork for the removal of a provision that, in regard to some posts in the college, women had to retire on marriage; the statute requiring this was eventually revoked.[76] At its Annual General Meeting in 1980 the Federation passed a resolution 'To reword the Constitution [of IFUT]…so as to remove any wording which might suggest a differentiation between male and female members of the

---

[75] 'IFUT Presentation to National Education Convention', in *IFUT News*, vol. xvi (Winter 1993), pp. 1-2.
[76] IFUT Annual Report 1972, IFUT file R8.12.

Federation.⁷⁷ A Women's Committee was formed within the Federation in 1984:

> to deal with issues such as discrimination against women, promotion of women, child care facilities, women's pension rights, discriminatory interviewing practices, equal opportunity in education, women's studies programmes, etc.⁷⁸

The name of this committee was later changed to the Equality Committee. While the Equality Committee lapsed briefly towards the end of the 1980s, due largely to the involvement of its members in other areas and organisations concerned with similar matters, it was reconstituted in 1990 and has been very active since, conducting a survey on maternity leave among academics and producing a periodical entitled *Equality News* to keep IFUT members up to date on developments in regard to equality.⁷⁹ In 1994 IFUT affiliated to the National Women's Council of Ireland.⁸⁰

The submission made by IFUT to the Commission on the Status of Women in 1991 provides the best account of the Federation's policy on equality. In terms of employment, IFUT recommended equal provision for maternal, paternal and adoptive leave in all third-level institutions, adequate child-care facilities, opportunities to take career breaks with a guaranteed return to a full-time post, the appointment of

---

⁷⁷ IFUT AGM, 1980, IFUT file R8.22.
⁷⁸ IFUT Annual Report 1984, p. 19.
⁷⁹ IFUT Annual Report 1987, p. 18; IFUT Annual Report 1989, p. 5; IFUT Annual Report 1990, p. 11; *Equality News* (May 1991), p. 4.
⁸⁰ *Equality Issues* (Summer 1996), p. 11.

equality officers in universities and an overhaul of promotions policies to take equal account of teaching and research, as it was felt that research was weighted more heavily than teaching. This was seen to favour male academics, who were considered to focus more heavily on research, while women academics, it was believed, concentrated equally on both aspects. In order to encourage greater female interest in academia and university education, the Federation proposed a special system of grants for women post-graduates to increase the number of women in advanced study, encouragement of disciplines such as women's studies, and of greater participation by women at undergraduate level in traditionally male-orientated disciplines, such as engineering and veterinary medicine. For the benefit of both female staff and students, recommendations were put forward for policies such as the implementation of a programme to deal with sexual harassment.[81]

Having outlined the philosophy behind the Irish Federation of University Teachers, the activities undertaken by the Federation in seeking to give practical application to its principles will now be considered.

---

[81] IFUT's Submission to CSW, in *IFUT News*, vol. xii (Winter 1991/92), p. 12-14.

Part II - Activities

Industrial Relations

Salaries

The evolution of IFUT's role in salary negotiations has been outlined above, highlighting the importance of this consideration in the decision to form a trade union. The salary gains made by IFUT on behalf of Irish academics will be considered here. In 1972, prior to its establishment as a trade union and the acquisition of a negotiating licence, IFUT established a subcommittee, under Jim Dooge and Denis Lucey, to deal specifically with salaries. The first significant victory for this committee came in 1973 when it won a case in the Labour Court entitling assistant lecturers and equivalent to a 10% 'anomaly claim', in two phases of 5%. Initially, the Department of Education had sought to make this retrospective only to 1 January 1972. IFUT's case, heard in the Labour Court in May 1973, for a longer period of retrospection, was argued successfully by the Federation's delegation of Jim Dooge and Denis Lucey.[82] An important prerequisite to the hearing of this case was the establishment by IFUT of the right to be heard by the Labour Court. This case was also significant for establishing the principle of relativity between academic staff and appropriate general grades of

---

[82] The anomaly award was paid in two phases: 5% retrospective to 1 April 1971, and 5% retrospective to 1 October 1970.

the civil service, the achievement of which was one of the greatest successes of the salary committee.

Another important concession achieved in 1975 by IFUT was the application of the Devlin Pay Award in the civil service to higher academic grades in the five universities, which reinforced relativity between academics and civil service grades.[83] Increases were secured for staff in the dental schools in TCD and UCC in 1977 and 1978. From the late 1970s onwards IFUT has also dealt with relativity for higher technical staff, in which categories it has members in TCD. These victories proved very important in establishing the ability of the Irish Federation of University Teachers to negotiate successfully on behalf of its members for salary increases and brought recognition to the Federation as the body principally responsible for negotiating salary issues for university academics.[84]

All the relativities in question have been maintained through the 1980s and '90s. Non-academic professionals who have joined IFUT, such as librarians and administrators, have also benefited from these relativities. In addition to the campaigns for salary adjustment, action has been undertaken to secure proper practices of scale placement on recruitment

---

[83] The Devlin award entitled those eligible to a 3.4% increase, with effect from 1 June 1974.

[84] Interview with Jim Dooge, 9 February 1999; Annual Report, 1973, IFUT file 8.14; Secretary's report, 1974, IFUT file R8.16; Labour Court, *Recommendation No. 3018: University Colleges Cork, Dublin & Galway and Trinity College, Dublin - Applications of Anomaly Award to Full-time Academic and Administrative Staffs*, 5 July 1973; Secretary's report, 1974, IFUT file R8.16.

and promotion. Moreover, improvements in pay for extra work, such as evening lectures and exam marking, have also been negotiated successfully.

A major task inherited in 1980 by the new General Secretary, Daltún Ó Ceallaigh, was gaining the acceptance of a new relativity for the Colleges of Education, resulting from the introduction of the new Bachelor of Education degree in 1974. This was achieved in December 1980 when the existing RTC relativity was broken and a new one put in place with the then Thomond College, thus giving very substantial increases in salary.[85] Follow-throughs to this action entailed bringing the colleges' exam payments into line with NUI norms and the introduction of a new top grade of Principal Lecturer, the equivalent of Associate Professor.

In the mid-1980s, an important development was the securing of a Labour Court recommendation against the so-called '60/40 ratio'. This refers to a policy of the Higher Education Authority whereby no more than 40% of full-time academic posts or equivalent were supposed to be at what is called 'senior' level - the Senior Lecturer, Associate Professor and Professor grades. As the demographic profile of academic staff by that time was revealing a bunching at the top of the College Lecturer scale, this had led to a severe restriction on promotional opportunities beyond that level.

Throughout the period from 1970 to the present, IFUT has acted on behalf of members in securing the relevant increases due to them under the various national pay schemes,

---

[85] *IFUT News*, vol. iv, no. 1 (Spring/Summer 1981), p. 1.

such as the National Wage Agreements, Agreement on Pay in the Public Service, Public Sector Pay Agreement, Programme for National Recovery, Programme for Economic and Social Progress, Programme for Competitiveness and Work, and the current Partnership 2000 programme.

Conditions of Employment

As outlined previously, one of the principal objectives of the Irish Federation of University Teachers is the protection of the terms and conditions of employment of its members. In a number of instances this has led IFUT to resort to both legal and industrial action to defend its members from dismissal or the threat of dismissal. A significant amount of IFUT's time is occupied with what are called 'personal cases'; that is, dealing with individual cases concerning salaries and conditions of employment. Other matters which have increasingly concerned IFUT in this regard include health and safety in its various forms regarding the working environment. In pursuit of its duty to protect the employment of its members IFUT has been involved in some high profile cases, which are described below.

(i) Maynooth Dismissals 1977

This case concerned two IFUT members, P.J. McGrath, Professor of General Metaphysics, and Malachy O'Rourke, a lecturer in the French Department. The dispute had its foundations in the decisions of both men to seek laicisation from the priesthood under the terms of the Second Vatican Council, one of the conditions of which was a prohibition on continuing to teach in 'a seminary, theological faculty or similar institution'.[86] The situation was complicated greatly by the dual status of Maynooth as a Pontifical University and a recognised college of the National University of Ireland. From IFUT's point of view the crucial issues of security of tenure and academic freedom were at stake, and the need for legislation to clarify the anomalous position of Maynooth was obvious.[87]

The dismissals of both men in May 1977 were the culmination of two years of disputation between themselves and the trustees of Maynooth, concerning their refusal to wear clerical garb or reside within the college.[88] IFUT's initial action was to impose a levy on its members to provide a support fund for the dismissed lecturers.[89] This was followed by a ballot on strike action in Maynooth, which voted 51 to 15 in favour of a one day stoppage on 9 May 1977. This was the first time since its achievement of trade union status that IFUT resorted to industrial action of any sort. There was disagreement within Council as to whether industrial or legal action was preferable. In support of the former it was argued that IFUT was failing as a trade union by not holding a national ballot on industrial action, whereas those who sup-

---

[86] P.J. Corish, *Maynooth College, 1795-1995* (Dublin: Gill & Macmillan, 1995), p. 382.

[87] President's address by Seosamh Hanly, 1977, IFUT file R8.19.

[88] A chronology of the events from 1974 to the dismissals in 1977 is provided in Justice Hamilton's High Court judgement on the case, reproduced verbatim in the *Irish Times*, 15 August 1978.

[89] Secretary's report, 1977, IFUT file R8.19.

ported the legal approach felt that the only form of industrial action which could be undertaken at that time of the year was exam disruption, which IFUT was in principle opposed to. In addition, it was felt that there would be difficulties in financing industrial action and in encouraging participation.[90] Council voted unanimously not to interfere with summer exams in any college, and by a narrow margin, 16 - 13, against holding a national ballot on industrial action. While the majority of Council favoured legal action, they did agree to have the posts 'blacked', recommending prospective applicants not to apply.[91] Initial legal steps failed when Mr. Justice Liam Hamilton refused a request for an injunction against the dismissals in June 1977. The next step was to take a case for unfair dismissal to the High Court, which was heard the following year. Apart from the division of opinion on whether industrial or legal action was preferable, there was also a body of opinion which felt that the Federation should not interfere in the case, an opinion was based on doubts as to the strength of IFUT's legal case.[92] According to Paddy O'Flynn, there was also opposition to involvement based on 'the belief that it was inappropriate for a body such as IFUT to challenge the authority of the hierarchy in the courts'.[93]

---

[90] Interview with Kieran Mulvey, former General Secretary of IFUT, 10 February 1999.
[91] Council minutes, 14 May 1977, IFUT file R8.39.
[92] Interview with Jim Dooge, 9 February 1999.
[93] Memo from Paddy O'Flynn, 21 April 1999.

In the meantime there was some dissent within IFUT concerning the action which the Federation had chosen to take in the case. Seven members signed a letter to the national newspapers outlining their opposition. When the Executive decided simply to reprimand, and not to expel them, Council objected that this was too lenient and asked the Executive to reconsider. However, the Executive refused to alter its decision.[94] Council and Executive clashed again over the blacking of the posts in Maynooth. In February 1978 Council unanimously reaffirmed its decision 'that no lectures or courses normally undertaken by [P.J. McGrath and Malachy O'Rourke]...be taken by IFUT members...'.[95] However, the continuation of this action was blocked by the Executive later that month:

> It was agreed after lengthy discussion of the situation that further blacking of posts would be neither useful or effective and that the decision on blacking should be referred back to the next meeting of Council for further consideration.[96]

The motion on blacking was duly rescinded by Council and in its stead a more modest motion was passed: '...to write to IFUT members in the Department of French and the Faculty of Philosophy instructing them not to carry out any extraordinary duties arising from the absence of Dr. McGrath and Mr. O'Rourke...'.[97] The more tolerant approach adopted by

---

[94] Executive minutes, 10 December 1977, IFUT file R8.40; Council minutes, 17 December 1977, 4 February 1978, IFUT file R8.41.
[95] Council minutes, 4 February 1978, IFUT file R8.41.
[96] Executive minutes, 25 February 1978, IFUT R 8.40.
[97] Council minutes, 11 March 1978, IFUT file R8.41.

the Executive was dictated by the fear of alienating members who might consider more severe action as too extreme.

The case brought by IFUT appealing against the dismissals was heard in the High Court in June 1978 before Mr. Justice Liam Hamilton. IFUT's legal team consisted of Donal Barrington, S.C., Hugh O'Flaherty, S.C. and Mary Robinson,[98] instructed by Gleeson, Mangan & Co. The trustees of Maynooth were represented by Rory J. O'Hanlon, S.C., John Blayney, S.C. and John Cooke, instructed by Arthur O'Hagan & Son.[99] The reasons which had been cited by the trustees for the dismissals included refusal to resign after laicisation, refusal to wear clerical garb, refusal to reside on campus, and in P.J. McGrath's case, publishing articles prejudicial to ecclesiastical authority without first seeking permission to publish from the trustees, as required by the college statutes.[100]

The general IFUT case was based on three arguments: firstly, the dismissals were considered to be invalid as the correct procedures had not been carried out in that the real reason for their dismissal was their decision to seek laicisation and not the charges alleged by the Maynooth trustees; secondly, dismissal on the grounds of laicisation was an infringement of both men's constitutional rights which amounted to discrimination on grounds of religious status; thirdly, the dismissal of McGrath, allegedly because of his

---

[98] Mary Robinson was a member of IFUT and later became President of Ireland. This is also true of President Mary McAleese.
[99] *Irish Times*, 8 June 1978.
[100] Ibid.

writings, was a breach of academic freedom and his constitutional right to free expresssion.[101] In regard to O'Rourke, it was argued further that his rescript of laicisation did not require his resignation, but even if it did, it would not be grounds for dismissing him from a publicly funded post. It was also argued that in his case the requirements for wearing clerical garb and residing on campus had been waived.[102]

The specific arguments made in support of McGrath's reinstatement were that the proceedings of the trustees amounted to invidious discrimination as the charges which they alleged were not *bona fide*; the resolutions for his dismissal were argued to be 'unreasonable, invalid and incompatible with the status of Maynooth as a Pontifical University and as a recognised college of the National University of Ireland'; dismissal was not deemed to be a penalty proportionate to the charges alleged by the trustees; and finally, it was argued that the proceedings of the trustees were invalid and a breach of constitutional and natural justice.[103]

Maynooth's chief defence centred on the college's status as a private corporation, the internal workings of which the civil courts had no right to interfere with. As such, the dismissals were claimed to be 'a *bona fide* exercise of the rights of the Trustees as laid down in the statutes of the college'.[104] In response to the charges made on behalf of the plaintiffs, that the trustees neither acted properly nor had the right to

---

[101] *IFUT News*, vol. ii, no. 8 (October 1978), p. 1.
[102] *Irish Times*, 8 June 1978.
[103] Ibid.
[104] *IFUT News*, vol. ii, no. 8 (October 1978), p. 1.

dismiss them, it was asserted that the trustees had complied fully with college procedures concerning dismissal, that the statutes of the college were legal and valid, that the trustees had acted within their statutory authority and that there was no legal basis for the High Court to consider the case.[105]

The judgement in the case was delivered by Mr. Justice Hamilton in August 1978. He found that laicisation was the real reason for the dismissal of both men. On this basis he felt that O'Rourke's dismissal was valid as he did not comply with the requirements of laicisation:

> In the case of Mr. O'Rourke...he had already applied for and been granted a rescript of laicisation which required him to resign his position. He had failed to comply with this requirement. The dismissal was carried out under the powers conferred on the trustees by the statutes and he was satisfied that they had followed the procedures laid down, said the judge.[106]

However, he found that the dismissal of McGrath was invalid, as the reasons cited for his dismissal - his writings and refusing to wear clerical garb - were not the real motives for his dismissal, that being his decision to seek laicisation:

> Dr. McGrath had not been laicised at the time of his dismissal, although he had applied for laicisation. Mr. Justice Hamilton said he was satisfied that the real reason for his dismissal was his laicisation application, and not the publication of writings prejudicial to ecclesiastical authority, or the failure to wear clerical garb, as cited by the trustees.[107]

---

[105] *Irish Times*, 8 June 1978.
[106] *Irish Times*, 10 August 1978.
[107] Ibid.

While Hamilton found that the dismissal of McGrath was invalid, he did not order his reinstatement, instead granting him damages of £9,966, commensurate with the loss sustained by him from the date of his wrongful dismissal in May 1977 until the date on which he could be validly dismissed, 24 November 1977, which was the date of his laicisation. He was also awarded 60% costs.[108]

In terms of the arguments which it had put forward on behalf of the plaintiffs, IFUT succeeded in establishing that the dismissals were directly related to their laicisation. Regarding the claim that the dismissals were in breach of the constitutional prohibition against discrimination on grounds of religious status, it was the view of Justice Hamilton that Maynooth's constitutional right to the full and free practice of religion was paramount.[109] The Hamilton judgement made no reference to academic freedom and did not consider the status of Maynooth as a recognised college of the NUI, in receipt of state funds, to be an overriding issue. Instead Maynooth's position as a seminary was clearly seen to be of greater importance, highlighting the centrality of the dual status of the college to this dispute:

> St. Patrick's College, Maynooth, was established for the purpose of educating persons professing the Roman Catholic religion...The fact that it is a college recognised by the National University of Ireland as providing courses of study of a university type does not alter its fundamental status and character...Neither, in my opinion, is its fundamental status and

---

[108] *IFUT News*, vol. ii, no. 8 (October 1978), p. 2.
[109] Ibid., pp. 1-2.

character affected by the fact that the State grants are available to it for the provision of secular education.[110]

On the advice of its legal counsel, and with the support of McGrath and O'Rourke, IFUT decided to appeal the Hamilton judgement to the Supreme Court, to seek the initial desire of having both men reinstated.[111] Some members, including the President and Honorary Secretary - Paddy O'Flynn and Caroline Hussey - were apprehensive about the consequences of the decision to appeal the original ruling.[112] In appealing the case, IFUT was particularly concerned with establishing 'a definitive legal determination of the status of St. Patrick's College Maynooth and the rights of our members in that institution'.[113] The case was not listed for hearing in the Supreme Court until the end of 1979. In the meantime O'Rourke had secured employment with the EEC in Brussels, but McGrath had been unable to find an alternative academic position in either Ireland or Britain and the IFUT benefit fund was only able to pay him maintenance until the end of June 1979.[114]

The Supreme Court delivered its judgement on the appeal in November 1979. In the case of O'Rourke,

---

[110] *Irish Times*, 15 August 1978.
[111] Executive minutes, 9 September 1978, IFUT file R8.40; Council minutes, 14 October 1978, IFUT file R8.41.
[112] Memo from Paddy O'Flynn, 21 April 1999.
[113] *IFUT News*, vol. ii, no. 8 (October 1978), p. 1.
[114] Ibid., vol. iii, no. 10 (Autumn 1979), p. 7; Executive minutes, 4 May 1979, IFUT file R8.42; Council minutes, 22 September 1979, IFUT file R8.43.

The Court unanimously affirmed Mr. Justice Hamilton's ruling that Mr. O'Rourke was dismissed from office for being in grave delinquency against clerical obligations in insisting in teaching in the college after his laicisation when the rescript of laicisation contained a condition that he was not to teach in a seminary, the college being essentially a seminary.[115]

However, in an unexpected move, the court unanimously overturned Hamilton's verdict that McGrath had been dismissed for a reason other than those cited by the trustees:

> that he was validly dismissed from office for being in grave delinquency against clerical obligations, contrary to the statutes, in refusing, in breach of canon law and despite having been requested to do so, to wear clerical dress in the college.

In addition, the Chief Justice (Mr. Justice O'Higgins) and Mr. Justice Griffin felt that McGrath's dismissal was lawful 'because, in breach of the statutes of the college, he had published three articles which were prejudicial to ecclesiastical authority and the interests of the college'.[116] The decision to appeal the original judgement to the Supreme Court was a risk which did not pay off, leaving the plaintiffs and IFUT in a worse situation that they been in after the initial case in the High Court. Following this blow it was decided not to proceed with a case under the Unfair Dismissals Act.[117] Although it was reported in 1980 that Mary Robinson was considering an appeal to the European Court, this option does not appear to have been followed through.

---

[115] *Irish Times*, 2 November 1979.
[116] Ibid.
[117] Executive minutes, 15 December 1979, IFUT file R8.44.

The Maynooth case was clearly a defeat for IFUT. Those who had initially favoured industrial action in preference to the legal option still felt that more could have been achieved if that route had been chosen. Divisions within IFUT had been revealed. The choice of legal rather than industrial action may have been an indication that IFUT had not yet become fully comfortable with the implications of its status as a trade union. Council and Executive were also at odds, as seen from their disagreements over the continued blacking of posts in Maynooth and the treatment of the members who dissented publicly from IFUT's policy in regard to the case. The case had also dominated the work of the entire federation for nearly three years, to the detriment of its work in other areas, and some members unhappy with the Federation's actions had resigned. Aside from the organisational implications, the case had also been a setback in terms of one of IFUT's chief policy aims as the vexed question of the exact status of the recognised NUI college at Maynooth vis-à-vis the seminary remained, if anything, more intractable.

However, the General Secretary at the time, Kieran Mulvey, feels that the experience did have some benefits for the Federation. In particular, he stresses the importance of the fact that the organisation remained solid, and while there may have been some defections, these were not whole-scale. Taking the case in the first place was proof that the infant trade union 'was willing to fight the hard battle'. He also points to the significance of the case in establishing the right of IFUT to represent dismissed members and to have such a case heard in the courts.[118]

(ii) Mary FitzGerald

At the height of the controversy between IFUT and Maynooth, another incident took place which exacerbated the dispute between both parties. This was the decision not to reappoint Mary FitzGerald to a lecturing post in the English Department at Maynooth in 1978. The decision of the trustees not to renew Ms. FitzGerald's contract was a very surprising action, as she had been recommended for a permanent post by a board of independent assessors, the arts faculty of the college and the academic council in Maynooth. She also had the support of Peter Connolly, head of the English Department in Maynooth at that time.[119]

No specific reasons were cited by the trustees for refusing to sanction the reappointment. The General Secretary of IFUT, Kieran Mulvey, expressed concern at the possibility that 'considerations other than her academic ability may have influenced the college authorities in turning down Miss FitzGerald for the post', in particular he felt that her 'married status' and her role as secretary of the Academic Staff Association in Maynooth at the time of the legal dispute between Maynooth and IFUT over the dismissals of P.J.

---

[118] Interview with Kieran Mulvey, 10 February 1999.
[119] Christina Murphy, 'Post refused to FG leader's daughter', in *Irish Times*, 30 June 1978.

McGrath and Malachy O'Rourke, may have been factors in the decision not to reappoint her.[120]

While IFUT's lawyers felt that a case could be brought to the Equal Employment Agency on grounds of marital discrimination, it would be preferable to take it to the Employment Appeals Tribunal, seeking Ms. FitzGerald's reappointment.[121] An offer by Maynooth for an out of tribunal settlement had been rejected by the Federation.[122] In this case the decision went against Maynooth, although while the tribunal found that she was unfairly dismissed it did not order Ms. FitzGerald's reinstatement, which it felt would be impractical, or a damages award. In any event she had found alternative employment in UCD.[123] An appeal against this finding was not considered to be in the best interests of either IFUT or Ms. FitzGerald.[124] It was probably unwise to risk a repeat of the reversal of the McGrath judgement.

(iii) Carysfort

Another major event in which IFUT became involved to protect the employment of its members was the closure of Our Lady of Mercy College of Education in Carysfort.[125] The

---

[120] *Daily Telegraph*, 10 July 1978, IFUT file 2.2.
[121] Executive minutes, 7 July 1978, IFUT file R8.40.
[122] Interview with Kieran Mulvey, 10 February 1999.
[123] Secretary's Report, 1979, IFUT file R8.21; *IFUT News*, vol. ii, no. 9 (1979), p. 5.
[124] Council minutes, 22 September 1979, IFUT file R8.43.
[125] A prestigious IFUT member here had been Séamus Heaney, later awarded a Nobel prize for literature.

shock announcement of the Carysfort closure was made on 4 February 1986. The then Taoiseach, Garret FitzGerald [126], outlined the reasons for the decision in his memoirs:

> In view of the impending rapid decline in the number of primary pupils - due to fall by some 135,000, or almost 25 per cent, by the end of the century - a decision we had to take in Government was to close one of the training colleges for primary teachers, Carysfort College in Dublin. There was already considerable overcapacity in the system; before the end of the 1980s the remaining training colleges would have four times as many places as would be needed.[127]

The closure did not come as a surprise to the leader writer in the *Irish Times*, who felt that:

> anyone who had been carefully watching educational trends could have read the writing on the wall. Birthrates are falling rapidly, intake into the colleges of education had fallen by almost one-third, and it is estimated that the primary school population will fall by some 80,000 over the next few years.[128]

The closure also came in the middle of a severe economic recession, a time when one of the first moves a government makes is to cut back on the number of public service employees, including teachers. Job opportunities for newly-

---

[126] Incidentally, Garret FitzGerald was a member of IFUT at the time of the Carysfort closure. He had been in the Federation since his time as a lecturer in economics in UCD in the 1960s, and he remains a member in the 'retired' category. His membership of IFUT made him the first Taoiseach to be in an ICTU-affiliated trade union.

[127] Garret FitzGerald, *All in a Life: an autobiography* (Dublin: Gill & Macmillan, 1991), p. 621.

[128] *Irish Times*, 6 February 1986, editorial.

trained teachers were also curtailed by factors such as a decline in the number of retirements from the profession, due in part to women continuing in their teaching posts after marriage.[129] The decision to close Carysfort in particular was dictated to a certain extent by geographical factors:

> It would have been impossible to close Limerick, the only college outside Dublin; the only Church of Ireland College couldn't go either, neither could Marino, the only college training teachers entirely through Irish. St. Pat's is on the north side of Dublin - badly served by third level colleges already - it is bigger than Carysfort and it has an educational research centre attached to it. Closing Frobel would have saved little money. So the axe fell on the oldest and possibly most renowned of the colleges.[130]

In her cabinet diaries published four years later, the Minister for Education with responsibility for the closure, Gemma Hussey, described the move as 'a political disaster of amazing proportions',[131] which indeed it turned out to be as successive governments were forced to honour the employment rights of the former Carysfort staff, whose case was led by IFUT.

The first response of the Irish Federation of University Teachers to the closure of the college, where practically all of the staff were among its members, was a press statement in which it 'rejected the proposal to close Our Lady of

---

[129] Christina Murphy, 'Carysfort a victim of falling roles', *Irish Times*, 6 February 1986.
[130] Ibid.
[131] Gemma Hussey, *At the cutting edge: cabinet diaries, 1982-1987* (Dublin: Gill & Macmillan, 1990), p. 196.

Mercy College of Education, Carysfort, and expressed its determination to resist the move'. In the statement IFUT outlined its fears for the implications which the closure would have on the already unsatisfactory teacher-pupil ratio, the quality of primary teaching and the employment prospects of young people wishing to become teachers. It concluded by deploring 'the brutal lack of consultation in relation to the proposed measure and the inept and insensitive manner of its announcement'.[132]

This action was followed by a demand for an immediate meeting with the Department of Education. Following an unsatisfactory meeting with officials on 5 February, a demand for another meeting with the departmental secretary was successful. Meetings were also held with the Sisters of Mercy, who ran the college, and the Archbishop of Dublin, and sought with all political leaders. Aside from such numerous meetings, plans were assembled for a campaign of public lobbying against the closure and a memorandum was drawn up outlining the potential which Carysfort had for alternative use. As a result of the negative reaction which greeted the closure, from a wide range of bodies within Irish society aside from IFUT, the new Minister for Education, Patrick Cooney, who had replaced Gemma Hussey, an immediate political casualty of the decision, announced that the government would keep the college open in some form, resulting in the appointment of a ministerial working party to

---

[132] IFUT press release on the proposed closure of Carysfort, 5 February 1986, IFUT file 11.16(II).

decide on the future of Carysfort.[133] Nothing materialised from this proposal and Carysfort was eventually closed and bought in controversial circumstances by University College Dublin.

In his address to the Federation's Annual Delegate Conference in 1986, the year in which the closure was announced, the President, John Lewis, revealed that it had soon become clear to IFUT following its meetings with the Department of Education in February that no contingency plans existed for the future of Carysfort. He also felt that IFUT, by its prompt action in objecting to the move, had succeeded in heading off a scheme to close the college that year.[134] Instead the department timed the closure for the end of the 1987-88 academic year, in order to allow first year students in 1985-86 to complete their degree course.

A large part of IFUT's time and energy over the next few years was taken up with discussions with government concerning the future of the 54 Carysfort staff. A voluntary redundancy scheme introduced in the civil service in 1987 to help achieve public service cutbacks was extended to allow Carysfort staff to avail of it. As only a few chose this option IFUT fought for redeployment to other colleges or other areas of the public service.[135] At one stage in early 1988, as the closure of the college in June of that year approached, it seemed as if IFUT would have to institute legal proceedings to prevent the government from making the Carysfort staff

---

[133] IFUT Annual Report 1986, p. 10.
[134] Ibid., p. 22.
[135] IFUT Annual Report 1987, p. 16.

redundant. However, the Minister for Education in the new Fianna Fáil minority government, Mary O'Rourke, assented to IFUT's demands for 'redundancy purely on a voluntary basis, reasonable redeployment, or continuation of salary until such time as the latter had been arranged'. By the time the Annual Delegate Conference of IFUT was held in 1988, the situation with regard to the 54 Carysfort staff was that 5 had opted for voluntary redundancy, 7 had gone to other Colleges of Education, 14 to other third-level colleges, while provision had been made for 2 more outside of either the voluntary redundancy or redeployment processes. Plans were in progress for the redeployment of 15 more, which would leave 11 unaccounted for.[136] By 1990 efforts were still ongoing to accommodate these remaining 11 members of staff, 9 of whom were academic and 2 non-academic - a nurse and a librarian. Plans to integrate the 11 academic staff into the inspectorate of the Department of Education were being opposed vigorously by civil service trade unions.[137] This dispute was finally resolved allowing the remaining academic staff to take up positions in the department. The librarian was moved to a post in the National Library and the nurse accepted an improved redeployment offer.[138]

The Carysfort campaign was a protracted one for IFUT. It took five years, from the announcement in 1986 that the college would be closed, until 1991, to make alternative employment provisions for the Carysfort staff. The campaign

---

[136] IFUT Annual Report 1988, p. 20.
[137] IFUT Annual Report 1990, p. 9.
[138] IFUT Annual Reports 1990-1992, p. 10.

did not lead to Carysfort being kept open as a College of Education. However, IFUT did have an important victory - the establishment of the principle of tenure. IFUT defines tenure as a fixed-term contract to the age of 65 and thus as distinct from 'permanency', whereby a job is guaranteed to age 65 *subject to demand*. Having effectively recognised that tenure applied to the staff in Carysfort, the government could not simply make them redundant when the college closed, as tenure would arguably have entitled the staff to payment for the duration of their contracts until they reached 65.[139] The principle of tenure was later given legal status in the 1997 Universities Act as a result of successful lobbying by IFUT.

(iv) TCD Attempted Dismissal 1992-93

The last major case in which IFUT became involved to protect a member from dismissal occurred in Trinity College in 1992/93, when the college attempted to remove a tenured academic in a clinical area, allegedly on grounds of incompetence. Negotiations which had taken place during the previous year between the Federation and TCD had not prevented the suspension of the staff member concerned at the beginning of the 1992/93 academic year. IFUT immediately instigated preliminary High Court proceedings which had the effect of forcing the board of Trinity College to set itself up as a tribunal to investigate the case. *IFUT News* later de-

---

[139] Interview with Daltún Ó Ceallaigh, General Secretary of IFUT, 7 December 1998.

scribed the proceedings as a hearing conducted 'according to the standards virtually of a criminal trial'. IFUT brought in a senior counsel (Michael McDowell), a junior counsel and a solicitor to collaborate with the General Secretary in the conduct of the case. The outcome of the process was a decision by the board of Trinity College that no case for dismissal existed. What did emerge were differences of opinion about clinical practice and, indeed, a certain tension between primacy in the aims of teaching and treatment as well as interpersonal difficulties. The case was a significant victory for the Federation; according to *IFUT News*:

> This was an historic episode and proved the necessity of having the Irish Federation of University Teachers to protect tenured academics at a time when increased pressure is being put upon them generally and in particular in regard to security of employment.

Another important lesson which the Federation learned from this episode was 'the requirement of having a good Contingency Fund which allows for this kind of action'.[140]

Response to Government Policy on Higher Education

UCD/TCD Merger

Not long after its foundation IFUT was faced with the prospect one of the most radical changes ever proposed in higher education legislation in Ireland - the plan by the then Minis-

---

[140] All the above information, including quotations, is derived from *IFUT News*, vol. xiii (Winter 1992/93), p. 2.

ter for Education, Donagh O'Malley, to merge University College Dublin and Trinity College Dublin into one single University of Dublin. An investigation of the future of the National University of Ireland and Trinity had been part of the remit of the Commission on Higher Education because by the 1960s it was clear that some changes would need to be made to the structure of both institutions if they were to cope with the rapid changes taking place within Irish higher education. A sustained increase in participation at second-level was leading to demands for increased access to tertiary education. The need for change was outlined by Donal McCartney of the UCD History Department in a pamphlet on the merger published by the UCD Academic Staff Association in 1967:

> And so in 1967 changing circumstances, including the greater demands for university education, the State's plans for post-primary and post-secondary education, the relative decline in Trinity's financial resources forcing it to seek state aid to an extent unknown before in its history, the effect of the Vatican Council on Catholic attitudes, and the need for rationalization, have all helped to re-open once more the whole question of university education.[141]

The solution proposed by the Commission on Higher Education was to abolish the NUI: '...the NUI system should be dissolved and its three constituent colleges be reconstituted as separate and independent universities...'. Significantly, the report specifically discouraged any sort of merger of the

---

[141] Donal McCartney, 'Historical Survey, 1592-1908', in *The Proposed Merger with TCD* (Dublin: UCD Academic Staff Association, 1967), p. 9.

two Dublin universities: 'Nor is it opportune to contemplate associating UCD and TCD either as two colleges in a federal university or incorporating them in a single university'.[142] O'Malley's plan, therefore, was directly contrary to the recommendations of the Commission on Higher Education.

The merger plan, which was formulated by O'Malley in advance of the publication of the Commission's report in 1967, was clearly intended to pre-empt those aspects of the report relating to Trinity and UCD, which did not correlate with the plans which the Minister had for the future of the country's two largest universities. According to O'Malley there were two chief reasons for his proposed action - financial and educational - which he outlined to a meeting of the UCD Academic Staff Association in July 1967, three months after he made his initial statement announcing the proposal:

> We, the Government, were faced with repeated capital charges running into millions with every indication that with pressure for university places such claims were only beginning. Something, therefore, had to be done in relation to the competitive element, and there must in any case be some form of new university set-up, and the time seemed ripe for a decision which should have been taken a long time ago.
>
> The financing of our university institutions has been a developing problem. It is true that in the matter of buildings, University College had to be catered for and pretty fast. If the Government had not taken action in that regard, many of you would be giving lectures and practicals in the street. TCD and its rising population had not an unreasonable capital claim.

---

[142] *Summary of the Report of the Commission on Higher Education* (Dublin, Stationery Office, 1967), Chapter 15: Future of the NUI, p. 48.

The Government was plunging with its eyes wide open into a morass of duplication to which no-one could foresee the end...[143]

When he first announced the merger plan in April 1967, O'Malley cited as a reason for it his desire 'to put an end to what he described as "a most insidious form of partition on our own doorstep" '.[144] He elaborated on this, the educational reason for the merger, in his meeting with the UCD ASA in July:

> Competition between universities and the brain-drain generally are rendering it extremely difficult to improve the quality of academic staff and that is putting it mildly. We are going to need more academic staff here and we are going to find it harder to recruit them, at least out of the scholarship and teaching power that are available to us. Perhaps even more important than this is something that is obvious on the side line but may not be so easily perceived from within the colleges. This is the undesirable effect on students minds of the partition of two universities in the same city.[145]

Not surprisingly, the O'Malley plan immediately encountered opposition from the two universities involved. This opposition was based in large part on the fear that the motivation behind the scheme was to bring universities under more direct state control.[146] In his autobiography, Garret

---

[143] Address by the Minister for Education, Donagh O'Malley, to the UCD ASA, 12 July 1967, UCDA, Edwards papers LA 22/311.
[144] *Irish Times*, 19 April 1967.
[145] O'Malley to UCD ASA, 12 July 1967, UCDA, Edwards papers LA 22/311.
[146] Interview with Val Rice, 25 February 1999.

FitzGerald, who was an economics lecturer in UCD at the time, recounted how the UCD authorities had:

> apparently got wind of what the Minister intended to do...and...decided to pre-empt it by publishing a merger proposal of their own. This proposal would have the effect of submerging TCD totally in UCD by means of a complete merger of every individual faculty and department: UCD, being the larger college, would have had a majority of staff in almost every merged unit. The minister in turn apparently learned of this UCD establishment ploy and instead suggested 'one University of Dublin, to contain two colleges, each complimentary to the other' - wording that did not fit in with the UCD authorities' 'total merger' concept.[147]

Although planning to combine the resources of both institutions, O'Malley wished for each to retain its distinctive identity within the new alliance.[148] While the majority of the academic staff in UCD were not in support of this plan by the authorities of their college, according to FitzGerald, they were still 'divided on the merits of a merger'.[149]

O'Malley outlined his plan for the governance of the new combined university to a meeting of the governing body of UCD in June 1967. The university was to have an overall 'University Authority' comprising of representatives from UCD, TCD and the government. Some of the most popular subjects would be available on both campuses, but there would be streamlining of the smaller faculties, with most of

---

[147] FitzGerald, *All in a Life*, p. 81.
[148] Statement by Donagh O'Malley to the governing body of UCD, 1 June 1967, UCDA, Edwards papers LA 22/311.
[149] FitzGerald, *All in a Life*, p. 81.

the professional ones - medicine, veterinary, law, architecture, dentistry, commerce and agriculture - being located solely in Trinity.[150] The Minister was adamant that there would 'no denominational basis' for the new university. Clearly it was his aim to put an end, by legislative means, to the church imposed prohibition on the attendance of Roman Catholics at Trinity College, which was a cause of much embarrassment by the late 1960s. This was also part of O'Malley's declared aim to end the 'insidious partition' of the two universities.

IFUT shared O'Malley's desire that the Trinity ban be abolished. Catholic academics in Trinity were particularly unhappy at the restriction. In 1969 Council appointed a sub-committee to examine 'the evidence for the allegation of the Catholic Hierarchy regarding the danger to faith and morals in attending TCD, and...the effects of the ban and the possible effects of its removal'.[151] The report of this subcommittee, entitled *Catholics and Trinity College*, which was published in January 1970, considered the ban to be unjustified, being unconvinced 'that the atmosphere of Trinity College is less favourable to Catholic faith and morals than that of any other Irish university institution'. The report condemned the inconsistency of the Catholic hierarchy for claiming 'that Catholic students at Trinity College do not receive a Catholic intellectual and moral formation', while prohibiting a Catholic chaplaincy at the college which might have helped

---

[150] O'Malley to UCD governing body, 1 June 1967, UCDA, Edwards papers LA 22/311.
[151] IFUT Annual Report 1969, IFUT file R8.9.

to provide such services.[152] On the basis of this report, IFUT Council issued a press statement calling on the hierarchy to remove the ban and provide a chaplaincy service for Roman Catholic students in Trinity.[153] Not long afterwards, in 1970, the ban was revoked, and it is a widely-held view within IFUT that the report was influential in its removal.[154]

IFUT did not respond immediately to the Minister's statement announcing the merger in April 1967, waiting instead for the outcome of a conference of its members on the issue in mid-July of that year.[155] Following this conference the Council of IFUT prepared a document entitled *The Proposed University of Dublin*, which was presented to the Minister on 22 September 1967. This paper declared IFUT's overall opposition to O'Malley's proposed scheme:

> ...the Council of IFUT does not commit itself to the view that the Minister's proposal forms the best solution to the problem of co-ordinating the work of the two Dublin Colleges with each other and with the other Irish Colleges.

However, accepting that O'Malley intended to effect his plan in some form, the policy document outlined IFUT's views on the proposed university in four categories. Firstly, under the heading of 'The concept and essential attributes of

---

[152] *Catholics and Trinity College*, January 1970, IFUT file 5.21.
[153] IFUT press release on TCD ban, 21 March 1970, IFUT file 11.16(I).
[154] Interview with Val Rice, 25 February 1999; memo from Paddy O'Flynn, 21 April 1999.
[155] AGM minutes, 29 May 1967, IFUT file R8.7.

the University of Dublin and the constituent colleges', it expressed the desire that

> each college should contain an adequate range of Arts, Science, and Professional subjects without which it would not be possible for either College to provide the nucleus of a real academic community, or to retain what is valuable in its identity and traditions.

The second aspect of the merger which particularly concerned IFUT was 'the principles to be followed in determining what subjects shall be taught in each College'. While recognising that there was a genuine need for streamlining, IFUT warned that 'the principle of avoidance of duplication' should not be the sole criterion for judging this, but that a number of factors should be taken into consideration; these included: a decision on what constituted the basic or essential subjects which should be continued in both colleges, economic considerations, the necessity for having an adequate range of teaching staff in all teaching areas, the maintenance of student numbers within manageable boundaries, the maintenance of inter-disciplinary links, the relationship of certain subjects to particular cultures or traditions and the views of the academic staff.

In establishing the 'structure of the relationships between the University of Dublin and its constituent Colleges', IFUT outlined a number of issues which would need to be defined clearly: the organisation of teaching in the university, procedures for the appointment of staff, maintenance of entrance standards, ownership of buildings and benefactions, the provision of finance and the composition of the governing bodies of each college and the overall university.

IFUT's final point referred to the 'relationship of the University of Dublin to the other existing Irish Colleges and to higher education in Ireland as a whole'. In this regard it was concerned that a giant new university would swamp the smaller colleges in Cork and Galway. To avoid this scenario IFUT sought a guarantee that adequate resources be given to these colleges to enable them to compete. In this regard IFUT put forward the suggestion that an investigation be undertaken to consider the feasibility of Maynooth also becoming a constituent college of the new University of Dublin.[156]

Following another conference on the subject of the merger, in 1968, IFUT focused more on its opposition to the merger than on seeking to accommodate it. In a second document, entitled *University Co-operation in Dublin*, published 2 November 1968, IFUT outlined its new policy of seeking co-operation between both universities without combining them in any form. It was the view of the Federation that the argument that there was too much unnecessary duplication of the courses in both universities, which was one of the chief reasons cited in favour of the merger, was exaggerated:

> In the main, our university resources are in use to their full capacity; indeed, by international standards, the level of utilisation of Irish university resources is remarkably high. Provided

---

[156] *The Proposed University of Dublin*, 22 September 1967, IFUT file 11.16(I).

student numbers are sufficient, there is not wasteful duplication if a subject is taught in both College Green and Belfield, any more than there is wasteful duplication if a subject is taught in a number of primary or secondary schools in the city.

The document proceeded to outline a number of existing factors which militated against both universities co-operating with each other. These included ecclesiastical restrictions, in the form of the Trinity ban; inequality of status, in that Trinity was a full university whereas UCD was only a constituent college of a university; the different structures of both colleges; and the rigidity of pension schemes which prevented free movement of staff between the colleges. IFUT did not believe that any of these obstacles were insurmountable.

The next step was to propose a scheme of co-operation which could be used as an alternative to the merger. In favouring co-operation over unity, IFUT stressed the importance of the autonomy of each college, which gave students a choice of academic traditions. The fear that a university which was too large would lead to students becoming alienated or anonymous was expressed: 'Even on grounds of numbers alone, we feel justified in fearing that the Government is about to create in Dublin a cumbersome and impersonal university monster'. The continuation of two separate universities, but with increased co-operation between them, was considered to be a much more natural solution to the problems in the university sector. The fact that this had been the recommendation of the Commission on Higher Education was also pointed out, as was the considerable level of opposition from academic staff in both universities to the merger proposal.

Having dismissed the duplication argument, the economic reasoning behind the merger - that one university would cost less than two - was similarly rebutted: 'there will be no significant saving in a combined University of Dublin that could not be achieved by a measure of rationalisation within the framework of two separate and co-operating universities'. Likewise, the social argument - the existence of the 'insidious partition' alluded to by Donagh O'Malley - was discounted on that basis that it was no longer true to assume that the student body of Trinity varied significantly from that of UCD, in other words it was no longer the case that one was Protestant and the other Catholic. The use of the merger scheme by the Minister as a means of getting rid of the Trinity ban was not seen as a legitimate reason for the plan: 'The argument that UCD and TCD should be made to suffer loss in order to secure the removal of the ecclesiastical restriction is unacceptable'.

In order to achieve a greater level of co-operation between UCD and Trinity, IFUT proposed that both should have equal status as full universities, there be mutual recognition of courses and exams, compatibility of term structure be introduced, formal arrangements be made for cross-registration, Catholics be permitted to enrol in Trinity without any restrictions and an interchangeable pension scheme be introduced for academic staff in both colleges. To co-ordinate such developments, and to encourage greater co-operation in higher education generally, the establishment of a Conference of Irish Universities was proposed. The IFUT document concluded by outlining why the plan for co-operation which it had produced was preferable to the full merger envisaged by Donagh O'Malley:

> Its implementation would require little disruption of work and few time-consuming administrative procedures. It is a plan which, we believe, will receive the support of the majority of the academic staff in both colleges, and, in the final analysis, no plan can work well without the convinced allegiance of the university teachers. This proposal offers a framework for the preservation of the educational values which have been achieved in TCD and UCD, whereas the single university proposal is fraught with danger of serious and permanent educational loss.
>
> A merger is likely to be an irreversible process; if it proves to be a mistake it will be very difficult to recover the ground which has been lost.[157]

The progress of the merger plan was delayed by the opposition which it encountered. From the government's point of view the merger appeared to be a very personal policy for Donagh O'Malley, and it is felt in some circles that it was his sudden death on 10 March 1968 which prevented the merger from ever being realised.[158] In addition, O'Malley had linked the merger to the ban on Catholics attending Trinity College, and it was felt that the removal of the ban in 1970 also removed much of the impetus for the merger.[159] The whole episode had proved to be very important for

---

[157] *University Co-operation in Dublin*, 2 November 1968, IFUT file 11.16(I).
[158] FitzGerald, *All in a Life*, p. 82.
[159] Interview with Val Rice, 25 February 1999.

IFUT. The Federation was in its infancy when faced with such a major challenge, but it did not falter in the face of it. Rather, the attempted merger proved to be an important factor in forging a sense of cohesiveness within the organisation; it was an opportunity for the members from the various colleges, especially UCD and TCD, to work together to prevent a development to which a large majority of them were opposed.[160]

1970s-1980s: Proposals for Higher Education Reform

Regardless of the failure of Donagh O'Malley's plan to merge UCD and Trinity College, the problem to which the merger had been proposed as a solution - the need to reform Irish higher education - remained. Throughout the 1970s various governments produced different proposals to deal with the situation. Initially in 1972, the Higher Education Authority, the intermediary body set up by the government in 1971 with responsibility for the funding and development of higher education, drew up a plan entitled *Reorganisation of University Organisation*, which to a large extent favoured the separate but co-operating universities alternative to the University of Dublin, which was favoured by IFUT and both universities, along with independent status for the universities in Cork and Galway.

However, as in the case of Donagh O'Malley's rejection of the recommendations of the Commission on Higher Education in this regard, the Minister for Education in the

---

[160] Interview with Paddy O'Flynn, 16 December 1998.

Fine Gael-Labour coalition government, Dick Burke, announced legislative proposals which were very different from the suggestions of the HEA.[161] It was envisaged that there would be three universities in the state: UCD, TCD and the NUI, which would consist of UCC and UCG. Maynooth was to be given the option of becoming a constituent of any of them. The proposed new technological college in Limerick - the National Institute for Higher Education (NIHE) - was also to become a college of the NUI, while its Dublin counterpart, which was already established, could join either of the Dublin universities. The majority of the members on the governing body of the NIHE colleges would be appointed by the government. While both of the Dublin universities were to be independent entities, the establishment of a conjoint board to co-ordinate their activities was proposed. A considerable rationalisation of facilities was also proposed: there were to be only two dental schools - in Cork and in Galway; UCD and Trinity were to have a shared science faculty, and the clinical medicine departments in both colleges were also to be merged; engineering, architecture, business studies, social science, agriculture and veterinary science were to be taught in UCD only, while dentistry and pharmacology would become the preserves of Trinity; arts, law and pre-clinical medicine would remain available in both universities.[162] In effect, this was the merger by stealth.

---

[161] John Coolahan, *Irish Education: its history and structure* (Dublin: Institute of Public Administration, 1981), p. 247.
[162] *IFUT News*, vol. ii, no. 2 (June 1975), pp. 19-20.

The only significant difference was the maintenance of the identity of both colleges.

IFUT objected immediately to the Burke plan, which, it believed, envisaged 'a greater degree of public control over institutions of higher education', thus diluting university autonomy; it was unable to see any virtue in the continued existence of the NUI structure. One particular focus of opposition was the plan to merge the science faculties of UCD and Trinity. A proposal to form a conjoint board 'to coordinate the two Dublin universities' was also objected to strongly.[163] A more detailed statement of the Federation's views on these proposals was issued in June 1975. This document recognised that there was a need for reform of Irish higher education and also for public accountability, but that this latter issue was not to be confused with bureaucratic control and that it should not infringe upon the principles of academic freedom and university autonomy. The belief that the NUI no longer served any purpose and should be abolished, to be replaced by five independent universities, was reiterated. In regard to rationalisation of the distribution of faculties, IFUT believed that there should be 'a gradual resolution of the problems that may arise over duplication and fusion of subjects and departments' and that, prior to any merger of departments, there 'ought to be an overwhelming economic case for fusion of faculties or subjects'.[164] Opposi-

---

[163] Press release with IFUT's initial response to the government's proposals, 22 December 1974, IFUT file 11.16(I); *IFUT News*, vol. ii, no. 2 (June 1975), pp. 6-7.

[164] 'Statement by the Irish Federation of University Teachers on the

tion to the Burke plan was also voiced by individual IFUT branches. In particular, the Maynooth Academic Staff Association felt aggrieved at the proposed retention of the NUI and issued a statement calling for independent university status for Maynooth.[165] The opposition encountered by the Burke proposals delayed the progress of their implementation. By 1976, over a year after they were initially announced, there was no sign of a white paper on them. The lethargy of the government was criticized by IFUT:

> Confusion and insecurity have become the dominant feature in most third level institutions. Mr. Burke's inertia has created chaos, piecemeal planning and ad hoc solutions for urgent problems. Long term planning within the universities has been held up, there is an overall lack of co-ordination and a disturbing tendency to change terminology in mid-stream so that 'proposals' become 'decisions' and any attempt to seek reasons for apparently arbitrary changes is presented as academic obstructionism.[166]

While the Burke proposals were never formally ratified and the plan was largely abandoned, some of the proposed faculty mergers were implemented. The most controversial of these was the decision to close the faculty of veterinary science in Trinity and confine the subject entirely to UCD. IFUT supported this move in principle:

Government's Proposals on Higher Education as announced by the Minister for Education on 16 December 1974', July 1975, IFUT file 11.16(I).
[165] *IFUT News*, vol. ii, no. 2 (June 1975), p. 16.
[166] Ibid, vol. ii, no. 4 (March 1976), pp. 2-3.

> The Council of the Irish Federation of University Teachers has consistently maintained that the improvement and progressive development of Veterinary education in Ireland was essential and that this could be ideally achieved by merging the two Schools of Veterinary Medicine in Dublin.[167]

However, the methods resorted to by the Minister for Agriculture, Mark Clinton, to effect the merger were a cause of much concern for both IFUT and the academic staff involved:

> Having apparently decided that it would take too long to wait for the "pre-legislative document" [white paper] and that his own area could be "tidied up" separately and without concern for the advancement of educational reasons, or for the balanced distribution of faculties between the Dublin colleges, Mr. Clinton has attempted to effect a merger of the Veterinary faculties of TCD and UCD...by the simple expedient of withdrawing funding from the TCD faculty and transferring it to UCD.[168]

As the Federation felt that the Minister was 'not concerned with educational objectives', and as he had virtually presented all involved with a *fait accompli*, the only grounds left on which to campaign for its members involved in the merger were those of salary, conditions of employment and status.[169] The government did meet a number of the demands of the academic staff involved - including guaranteed employment, maintenance of salary, pension rights, the right of some of the TCD staff to remain in that college within other

---

[167] IFUT press statement on the proposal to merge the vet. colleges, motion of IFUT Council, 11 October 1975, IFUT file 11.16(I).
[168] *IFUT News*, vol. ii, no. 4 (March 1976), p. 3.
[169] Secretary's report, 1976, IFUT file R8.18.

faculties. According to Tim Jackson, an IFUT member from the German Department in Trinity College, 'it is possible that IFUT can claim no credit whatever' for these concessions, although the Federation was instrumental in emphasising such demands. However, he indicated two distinct victories which were due entirely to the lobbying of IFUT. Firstly, an assurance was given that the new faculty would have much greater freedom of manoeuvre in regard to aspects such as finance. Secondly, a discrepancy in the drafting of the statutes for the new faculty regarding the designation of heads of department was discovered by IFUT and rectified.[170]

Rationalisation of faculties was also achieved at the same time in relation to both dentistry and pharmacology. The College of Pharmacy, which had links with UCD, now came under the aegis of Trinity, while dentistry courses in UCD, RCSI and UCG were closed and the students transferred to the only remaining dentistry schools in UCC and Trinity College. In both cases, as with the veterinary merger, IFUT was involved in negotiations on behalf of its members to secure their salaries and conditions of employment.[171]

Most of the Burke proposals were never implemented and were replaced in July 1976 with new plans for the establishment of Cork, Galway and Maynooth as independent universities. However, the coalition government was defeated before any serious developments in regard to this plan

---

[170] Tim Jackson, 'A Review of the Veterinary Merger - All Vets Together', in *IFUT News*, vol. ii, no. 6 (March 1977), p. 8.
[171] Secretary's report, 1977, IFUT file R8.19.

took place and a new government brought with it new ideas for reform of higher education. The Fianna Fáil government announced in 1977 that it had legislative plans for establishing four independent universities 'with reformed governing structures'. This excluded Maynooth, the status of which remained indefinite at a time when it was the cause of much debate due to the McGrath-O'Rourke case.

In a history of Irish education written in 1981, John Coolahan, predicted that 'It would seem that the early 1980s will see the long-delayed legislative reorganisation of Irish university education into five independent universities, with Maynooth offering a limited range of faculties'.[172] This was a reasonable assumption to make, given that reform had first been tackled in the 1960s with the establishment of the Commission on Higher Education. However, as the next decade and a half was to illustrate, it was an overly optimistic assumption.

Very few legislative proposals for restructuring of third level education were made during the 1980s. Government instability in the early years of the decade militated against any long term planning, but the principal deterrent was the poor state of the economy. Governments were more concerned with saving money by cutting back where possible. The closure of Carysfort, which has been examined earlier, was an example of this. Restrictions were also applied in regard to employment and university financing.

---

[172] Coolahan, *Irish Education*, pp. 247-8.

The only significant government initiative which concerned planning for the future of higher education was the *Education Action Programme, 1984-87*, produced by the Fine Gael-Labour coalition of the mid-1980s. IFUT's response to much of this document has been outlined in a previous section. This document referred to education in general, and where it referred to third level education it was more concerned with public accountability. The type of reforms needed within the university sector, in regard to university structure, planning for increased numbers of students, and allocation of faculties, which had been the focus of legislative proposals throughout the 1960s and 70s, were not central to the strategy outlined by the EAP.

1990s: Legislative Developments in Higher Education

In contrast to the decade which preceded it, the 1990s have witnessed some of the greatest changes in Irish higher education. It has been a period of unprecedented government action on education, with the production of a green paper and a white paper, the abolition of fees and the integration of Colleges of Education with universities and the enactment of the long-awaited legislation to restructure the universities.

The 1980s ended with the conferral of university status on the country's two National Institutes of Higher Education in Dublin and Limerick. In 1987 IFUT had prepared a detailed submission for the Minister for Education examining the arguments surrounding the transformation of these colleges into universities.[173] The next step in their expansion was a proposal to link the Colleges of Education, St. Patrick's in Drumcondra and Mary Immaculate in Limerick, with their neighbouring universities, Dublin City University and the University of Limerick. While the academic staff at Dublin City University and the University of Limerick were not members of IFUT - they remained in the Services Industrial Professional and Technical Union (SIPTU) and ASTMS (later MSF) respectively after their colleges acquired university status - the staff in both of the Colleges of Education were members of the APSCE division of IFUT. The rules of the Irish Congress of Trade Unions make it difficult for staff in DCU and UL to leave their own union to join IFUT.

During the negotiations on the linkages between both colleges IFUT represented its members in St. Patrick's and Mary Immaculate on a number of issues. In regard to the case of St. Patrick's, lobbying helped to secure full academic representation within DCU for the staff in St. Patrick's, a remission of fees for the children of St. Patrick's staff who were attending DCU and the acceptance of a sabbatical scheme similar to that in operation in DCU. A campaign for a separate academic council and governing body for the Drumcondra campus was also successful.[174] In the case of Limerick, the Federation helped to secure the involvement of its members in Mary Immaculate in the proceedings of the academic council and the governing body of the university.

---

[173] *A Technological University?*, 1987
[174] IFUT Annual Report 1994, pp. 12-3; IFUT Annual Report 1995, p. 14.

One of the most significant changes in Irish third level education during the 1990s was the abolition of university fees by the Labour Party's Minister for Education, Niamh Bhreathnach, a measure which had been a central issue in Labour's manifesto during the 1992 general election campaign. While IFUT welcomed the motivation behind this reform, to increase access to third level education, it was critical of claims that fee abolition alone would solve many of the problems in higher education. It argued that tuition fees represented only one aspect of the cost of higher education; other costs, such as maintenance, also restricted access to higher education and these barriers could only be removed by the introduction of a much more comprehensive system of grants. In addition to this, more resources would have to be provided to universities if the number of places in them were to be increased. IFUT was also concerned about the implications which fee abolition would have on the financing of universities.[175]

The coalition governments from 1992-1997 were undoubtedly the most active ever in regard to reform of the third-level sector. Although the Minister for Education throughout that period, Niamh Bhreathnach, was criticised widely by all sections of education, her activity with regard to legislation on education was in stark contrast to most of her predecessors. Apart from the measures described above, the Department of Education produced a green paper on education in 1993, a white paper in 1995 and held a national

---

[175] *IFUT News*, vol. xxi (Easter 1995), p. 5.

education convention also in 1993. One of the most important legislative results of these processes was the Universities Act of 1997, the first such piece of legislation since the act which established the National University of Ireland in 1908. This was the legislation which had been advocated by the Commission on Higher Education and promised by every government in the intervening thirty years.

When the intention to reform university structure, in particular the National University of Ireland, was announced by the Minister, IFUT set out a clear statement of its policy in that regard. The principal aspect of this policy was the view that the NUI structure should be abolished, a move which had been advocated by IFUT since it was recommended by the Commission on Higher Education. Another pressing issue was the status of Maynooth and the obvious need for a statutory separation of the seminary from the NUI college. Reform of the composition of the governing bodies of the NUI colleges was also sought, especially the abolition of local government representation. The Federation also believed that graduate representation on governing bodies should be abandoned as it was not seen as fulfilling any significant function and was being used by some staff to get representation by standing for election in their capacity as graduates; in its place a proper form of staff representation was proposed. As with governing bodies, IFUT sought reform of academic council structures, seeking a new form which would comprise all academic staff but with an executive committee to transact its routine business as, otherwise, a full academic council would be unwieldy. The full academic council, however, would retain control over academic policy. Another aspect of university governance which was believed to be in need of reform was the method of electing the university presidents; it was proposed that such appointments be made by the governing body of the university on the basis of wide-ranging consultation with academic opinion within the college. These proposals also envisaged greater independence for the NUI colleges; with the abolition of the NUI the powers of its senate should devolve to each of the colleges.[176]

When the universities bill was published on 30 July 1996 IFUT was dismayed by a number of its provisions. It felt that the proposed legislation 'seemed to involve a serious deterioration in terms and conditions of employment'. It also appeared to diminish the role of the Higher Education Authority as an intermediary between the government and the universities. The provisions which it contained in relation to the procedures for suspension and dismissal of academic staff were not considered to provide ample safeguards. As a trade union, IFUT opposed the prohibition on the nomination of staff to the governing bodies by outside institutions, including trade unions. The proposal for greater control of staff remuneration, which was now to be subject to ministerial approval, was also a ground for objection.

A clause which caused particular concern was the proposed deletion of section 3 of the 1908 Irish Universities Act, which prohibited the imposition of religious tests on

---

[176] Ibid, xiv (Spring 1993), pp. 1-4.

academics. The removal of this was suggested in an attempt to open the way for the teaching of theology as an academic subject and not as a means of instituting religious discrimination. IFUT's policy on the teaching of theology, which was formulated in a report in 1969 entitled *Theology in the University*, was that it should be taught as an academic subject outside any one particular church tradition, and thus it supported the intention of the government in regard to this aspect of the universities bill.[177] However, it was the possibility that the conditions for discrimination might be created by the abolition of section 3, albeit unintentionally, which caused concern.[178]

Following this announcement of its initial views on the proposed legislation, the Education Policy Working Group (EPWG) of IFUT set about preparing an in-depth analysis of the bill, which was produced in October 1996 in a document entitled *Universities Bill 1996 - Proposed Amendments*. This document served as the basis for the Federation's lobbying on seeking changes to the bill. One of the most intensive lobbying campaigns ever launched by IFUT, comparable only to its response to the Carysfort closure, was undertaken between October 1996 and the enactment of the bill in May 1997: meetings were held with senior civil servants in the Department of Education to explain the amendments being put forward by IFUT; an IFUT delegation outlined its concerns to the Dáil committee on social affairs; a meeting was

---

[177] *Theology in the University*, 1969.
[178] 'Initial IFUT response to the universities bill', in *Future of the Universities?*, 30 July 1996, pp. 23-24.

held with the Minister for Education; and the university senators were approached to secure some changes to the bill in the upper house.[179]

This document identified two main areas of objection in the proposed bill: 'The defects which we note in the Bill may be classified broadly into those which threaten the autonomy of the universities and those which drastically curtail the academic freedom of the staff in the universities'. To counter these, specific additions to the bill were proposed which would enshrine these sacrosanct principles of academic freedom and university autonomy; to section 12 the addition of the following sub-sections was proposed:

> (4) In the performance of its functions a university shall act at all times to maintain the academic freedom of its members.
> (5) In the performance of its functions, the right of a university to regulate its affairs in accordance with the traditions of university autonomy is recognised by this Act and nothing in this Act shall detract from the exercise of that right by any of the universities to which the Act applies.

A central aspect of university autonomy is the right of the university to appoint its own staff; IFUT again proposed additional subsections to have this principle enshrined in the bill. Likewise, a new subsection was suggested which would give the universities appropriate control over staff remuneration; this was proposed to replace the bill's original clause that all such expenses, fees and allowances be subject to ministerial approval.

---

[179] *IFUT News*, vol. xxiii (Winter 1996), p. 1; IFUT Annual Report 1997, p. 24.

Other proposed amendments sought to rectify what the Federation believed was a serious threat to the conditions of employment of academic staff, especially in regard to dismissal. An additional subsection was suggested which outlined clearly the grounds on which an academic staff member could be dismissed, a level of clarity not contained in the original bill:

> A university may not remove any officer from his or her office, except for failure to discharge the duties of such office. Prior to any such removal from office coming into effect, the person whose removal has been proposed may appeal against any such proposal to the Visitors, and the appeal shall be heard and determined in a manner provided in the charter of the university.

IFUT also proposed that procedures for dismissal should involve negotiations with trade unions and staff associations. Such proposed amendments clearly derived much from the experiences with Maynooth in the late 1970s and Trinity College in the early 1990s.

More specific proposals for amendment included representation for the academic staff of Mary Immaculate and St. Patrick's Colleges of Education on the governing authorities of the University of Limerick and Dublin City University respectively; guarantees of the rights of existing staff in universities; maintenance of section 3 of the 1908 act regarding the proscription of religious tests; various amendments to university charters; and the complete deletion of the restrictive section on academic evaluation.[180]

---

[180] All of the above information is contained in *The Universities*

While not all of IFUT's proposals were incorporated, the Minister was willing to accept a number of specific and significant changes based on the Federation's recommendations. The most important achievement was the establishment of an academic's right to tenure; academic staff were to be confirmed as 'officers' of the university, not merely 'employees', as the provisions of the original bill had stated. The importance of this recognition lies in the protection it gives to academic staff, allowing for their dismissal only in cases such as incompetence and unacceptable conduct. This provision conferred statutory status on the principle, enunciated at the time of the Carysfort closure, that tenured academics effectively have a fixed term contract to the age of 65. As a result of this clause, tenure for university academics in Ireland is now on a firmer footing than it had been under the previous act of 1908. Also in relation to conditions of employment, guarantees were secured to safeguard the existing rights of Maynooth staff under its new separate status as NUI, Maynooth. Equivalent provisions were made for staff in Colleges of Education, in the event of the incorporation of any such colleges into a university.

IFUT was also successful in having the principles of academic freedom and university autonomy, two of the main tenets of the Federation's philosophy, properly enshrined in the act. Securing legislative guarantee for these fundamental aspects of university culture has set a precedent, with uni-

---

Bill 1996 - Proposals for Amendment, 1996.

versity teacher organisations in other countries lobbying their governments for similar measures.

On the matter of section 3 of the 1908 act, relating to religious discrimination, the government had proposed the deletion of the entire section. A compromise was reached whereby only subsections two and three of the clause were deleted. Subsection one, which specifically outlawed religious tests remained; this stated that:

> No test whatever of religious belief shall be imposed on any person as a condition of his becoming or continuing to be a professor, lecturer, fellow scholar, exhibitioner, graduate, or student of, or of his holding any office or emolument or exercising any privilege in either of the two new universities, or any constituent college; nor in connection with either of those universities or any such constituent college shall any preference be given or advantage be withheld from any person on the ground of religious belief.

Areas in which changes sought by IFUT proved less complete included academic evaluation and the composition of governing bodies. The Minister refused to delete the provisions for academic evaluation, but did modify the proposals somewhat to take account of the concerns of the Federation; in particular, the term 'cost-effectiveness' was replaced and it was agreed that procedures for evaluation would be determined by the Higher Education Authority in consultation with the universities. In regard to the membership of university governing bodies, IFUT did not get local government representation eliminated, which is not very surprising as many members of the Oireachtas are also local representatives.

Other issues to which changes were secured included university charters and the visitorial system. It was agreed that trade unions were to be consulted in the course of preparing charters, which were to include provisions concerning equal opportunity for staff and students. In regard to the visitorial system for universities, the role of the High Court in the appointment of visitors was detailed.[181] Overall, IFUT was greatly satisfied with the changes which it had managed to secure, so much so that the detailed outline of the changes which had been made to the original bill was entitled *The Universities Act 1997 - IFUT Triumphs*!

International Activities

International Teacher Organisations

Having a dual status as both a trade union and a professional association, IFUT has forged many contacts, nationally and internationally, with organisations of both kinds. During the 1980s the Federation became involved in a wider European trade union organisation, associated specifically with education, the European Trade Union Committee for Education (ETUCE). IFUT has been a very active member of this committee, helping to develop its important and effective Higher Education and Research Standing Committee. IFUT has also been much involved in the work of the ETUCE Working Group on Teacher Education. In turn, the Federa-

---

[181] All of the above information is contained in *The Universities Act 1997 - IFUT Triumphs*, 22 May 1997.

tion has been drawn into meetings organised by the Trade Union Advisory Committee of the OECD. This is considered a valuable connection, given the role of the parent OECD in formulating and influencing international and national education policy.

Representatives of IFUT have also attended international conventions of organisations such as the World Federation of University Teachers' Unions and the World Trade Union Congress.[182] In 1993 two of the largest international bodies representing teachers' unions - the International Federation of Free Teacher Unions and the World Confederation of the Teaching Profession - merged to form a new movement called Education International (EI). IFUT was accepted as a member of this body and since then has attended regularly at its world conferences and those of its European regional section. During his time as president of IFUT, Eugene Wall gained a seat on the Higher Education Sectoral Committee of EI in 1995.[183]

ICUTO

In the early 1980s IFUT was involved in the evolution of the International Conference of University Teacher Organisations (ICUTO). This organisation brought together tertiary teacher organisations from Europe, North America, Africa

---

[182] IFUT Annual Report 1985, p. 4; IFUT Annual Report 1989, p. 31; IFUT Annual Report 1990, pp. 12-13.
[183] IFUT Annual Report 1993, p. 9; IFUT Annual Report 1994, p. 15; IFUT Annual Report 1995, pp. 16-17; IFUT Annual Report 1996, p. 14; IFUT Annual Report 1997, p. 15.

and the antipodes to examine problems common to university teaching throughout the world, such as terms and conditions of employment, access to university, research, international mobility of university teachers and mutual cooperation. In January 1985 a conference which was central to the evolution of ICUTO was hosted by IFUT in Dublin; it was attended by representatives from universities in 10 different countries.[184] Another ICUTO conference took place in Dublin in 1987. Throughout the years of its existence ICUTO issued a number of declarations. Of particular significance was its proposed *Recommendation on the Status of Higher Education Personnel*, which was drawn up in 1995. IFUT was actively involved in the drafting of this document, which was eventually adopted by UNESCO.[185] When ICUTO was being overtaken by the Higher Education section of Education International, Daltún Ó Ceallaigh produced *The Origins and Development of ICUTO, 1982-1996*. The involvement of IFUT in the construction of what was to become ICUTO developed soon after the termination of its membership of a similar organisation, the International Association of University Professors and Lecturers (IAUPL).

IAUPL and South Africa

IFUT joined the IAUPL during the academic year 1973-74 and played quite an active role in it. A significant aspect of

---

[184] IFUT Annual Report 1983, p. 14; IFUT Annual Report 1984, p. 9; IFUT Annual Report 1985, pp. 11-12; *The Origins and Development of ICUTO*, 1996, pp. 1-3.
[185] *ICUTO, 1982-1996: Documents*, 1996, pp. 45-50.

the Federation's activity in this organisation was Paddy O'Flynn's role as *rapporteur* in drafting what became the *Siena Declaration on Academic Freedom*. In 1981 IFUT was chosen to host a conference of the association in Dublin. Representations were made to the Federation by the Irish Anti-Apartheid Movement (IAAM), expressing concern that members of the University Teachers' Association of South Africa (UTASA) might attend, and requesting an assurance that they would not be allowed to do so. The IAAM claimed that UTASA had links with the apartheid regime in South Africa. At a meeting with the President, Vice-President and General Secretary of IFUT, the President of the Irish Anti-Apartheid Movement, Kader Asmal (who was also an active member and former President of IFUT) asserted that the South African association was linked to apartheid in that it worked within the apartheid framework at university level, had almost no non-white members and showed no signs of challenging apartheid in the South African education system. In addition to these reservations, the Association of University Teachers in Britain also made its opposition to the South Africans known. IFUT consulted with the Irish Department of Foreign Affairs, which reported that the United Nations Educational, Scientific and Cultural Organisation (UNESCO) was suspicious of the South African association and that racial discrimination was practised in the majority of South African universities. Based on this evidence IFUT refused to host the conference if the South Africans were to attend; the conference was duly transferred to Paris. The decision not to hold the conference in Dublin was based on

IFUT's strong anti-apartheid stance; at its Annual General Meeting in 1979 a resolution had been passed stating its opposition to apartheid in South Africa. The Irish Congress of Trade Unions, to which IFUT was affiliated, passed a similar motion.[186]

Adherence to this policy eventually brought about the sundering of IFUT's links with IAUPL. Arising out of the cancellation of the Dublin conference, the Federation pursued the issue of South African membership of the IAUPL, proposing that the expulsion of the South African association be considered. However, this stance received little support within the IAUPL, with Denmark being the only country openly to support the idea. As a result of the reluctance to address its concerns regarding South Africa and the continuation of South African membership, the Federation decided to disaffiliate from the IAUPL in 1982.[187] The Irish example was followed by the Danish university teachers' union and the AUT, both of which also withdrew.[188]

Opinion within the Federation had not been unanimous in regard to the South African episode. According to Paddy O'Flynn, a supporter of IFUT's membership of the IAUPL, some members questioned whether it was right to exclude the South African organisation, as it was considered to be representative of the more liberal, predominantly English-

---

[186] 'Memorandum on UTASA and IAUPL', 18 September 1981, IFUT file R8.47.
[187] IFUT Annual Report 1981, p. 11; IFUT Annual Report 1982, p. 11; Council minutes, 12 June 1982, IFUT file R8.50.
[188] *IFUT News*, vol. vii (Summer, 1984), p. 20.

speaking, section of white South African society. O'Flynn also believes that IFUT's disaffiliation was an unfortunate development, believing that the Federation had benefited much from its membership, in particular he highlighted the importance of the Sienna document on academic freedom which had bee drawn up by IAUPL.[189] This view of the beneficial nature of IAUPL membership was not shared by all IFUT members; Daltún Ó Ceallaigh has listed a number of reasons, other than the South African issue, for IFUT's decision to leave IAUPL, which are based on the view that it was no longer very effective:

> Firstly, the IAUPL was not particularly representative internationally, either from a continental or global point of view. Secondly, even within the countries concerned, the organisations in question very often did not appear to be particularly representative of university staffs. Thirdly, while it did do some useful work on the likes of academic freedom, the IAUPL was generally not a productive body.[190]

Opposition to apartheid led the Federation to affiliate to the IAAM in 1985.[191] This policy was reaffirmed at the following year's Annual Delegate Conference at which a resolution was passed recommending 'that IFUT members take no part in activities such as academic conferences, research projects, external examining, etc., which involve South African participants'.[192] As a direct result of this resolution, IFUT advised its members not to 'attend or assist in any

---

[189] Interview with Paddy O'Flynn, 16 December 1998.
[190] *The Origins and Development of ICUTO*, p. 1.
[191] IFUT Annual Report 1985, p. 14.
[192] IFUT Annual Report 1986, p. 23.

way' with a world computer conference which was scheduled to be held in Trinity College Dublin in September 1986. The Federation even went so far as to request the Minister for Foreign Affairs to use the Aliens Order to prevent any South Africans from entering Ireland to attend the conference. The basis for the intensity of opposition was the view that 'if South Africans attended, the conference would most likely assist, even if only indirectly, the repressive intelligence and military machines in their country'.[193] Since the fall of apartheid in the 1990s IFUT's relations with South Africa have been of a much happier nature, with the appointment of former IFUT President, Kader Asmal, as Minister for Water Affairs and Forestry in Nelson Mandela's government formed in 1994 and then as Minister for Education in the government of 1999.[194]

IFUT and the AUT

The Association of University Teachers is the United Kingdom's equivalent of IFUT, representing academics in Great Britain and Northern Ireland. When IFUT was being formed, the AUT was the model used by its founders. As the AUT is also a representative of university teachers on the island of Ireland, IFUT has sought to establish links with it to discuss matters of mutual concern. During his time as President in the early 1970s, Enda McDonagh endeavoured to establish stronger links between the organisations representing uni-

---

[193] News release, 1 August 1986, IFUT file 11.16(I).
[194] IFUT Annual Report 1995, p. 18.

versity teachers in the Republic of Ireland and Northern Ireland.[195] A formal arrangement for dialogue between the two organisations was started; in his report to the Annual General Meeting in 1971, the secretary, R. Conroy, outlined the proposals:

> It was agreed that meetings should be held at least once a term between representatives of IFUT and the Northern Ireland Colleges...it was also agreed that the Northern Ireland Colleges would take part in the Symposium Project and that the Secretaries of IFUT and the Northern Ireland AUT should make joint enquiries regarding university entrance requirements North and South of the border.[196]

Soon after these plans were made, the political situation in Northern Ireland was exacerbated by the Bloody Sunday killings of January 1972. In response to this event, the Council of IFUT sent letters of protest to *The Times* (London), *Die Welt* and *Le Monde*. In the annual report of IFUT's 1973 AGM, it was stated that the Federation had been 'unable to establish formal relationships with academic staff in Northern Ireland'.[197] Co-operation was boosted the following year when IFUT and the Northern Ireland AUT held a conference in Belfast on 'Co-operation between Irish Universities'.[198] Nevertheless, there is very little record of close association between both organisations from that time until the mid-1980s.

---

[195] Interview with Enda McDonagh, 22 February 1999.
[196] Secretary's report, 1971, IFUT file R8.11.
[197] Annual Report, 1973, IFUT file R8.14.
[198] President's address, 1974, IFUT file R8.16.

In 1985 links between the two unions representing academics on both sides of the border were reinvigorated. The impetus came from the establishment of a Northern Ireland Advisory Committee by the AUT and by the publication of the Williams' report on *Higher Education in Ireland: Co-operation and Complementarity*.[199] For the past decade a more solid association has been maintained between IFUT and the AUT in Northern Ireland, the high point of which were joint conferences held in Belfast in June 1997 and in Malahide, Co Dublin, in June 1998, which covered a wide range of university-related topics such as the expansion of higher education, university governance, new developments such as modularisation and semesterisation and more specific cross-border issues. IFUT has also been asked on occasion by the NIAC to attend its meetings and give briefings on the European trade union scene as regards higher education. During the 1990s IFUT has been involved in formalising links between teacher unions in Ireland and Britain through the mechanism of the British and Irish Group of Teacher Unions, which discusses education policy and strategy within European and global education union structures.

International Affairs

Aside from its involvement with other education organisations throughout the world, IFUT has always taken a keen interest in international affairs, especially those which involve education matters. In May 1984 IFUT, along with

---

[199] IFUT Annual Report 1985, pp. 11-12.

other teacher unions, passed a resolution condemning the decision of the National University of Ireland to award an honorary degree to the US president, Ronald Reagan.[200] A resolution adopted at the Annual Delegate Conference in 1986 deplored 'the decision to exclude Libyan students from entry to Ireland, which is in breach of the principle that bona fide scholars should not be prevented from travelling between countries in the pursuit of their studies'.[201] Following the suppression of the student demonstrations in Tiananman Square in 1989, IFUT extended its sympathy 'to the families and friends of its Chinese colleagues who died in the massacre in Beijing', and asked 'the Government of Ireland to make clear its abhorrence of the action of those now in power in the People's Republic of China'. A copy of this statement was sent to the Chinese Embassy.[202]

The development of such international links has been important to IFUT. The growth of the EU has had an impact on higher education in all of its member states, and as such it is important that Irish academics build up strong contacts with their European equivalents. Association with European and wider international university teacher associations has enabled IFUT to gain greater experience of world-wide trends in higher education, and provides a more extensive forum for participating in educational debate than is available in Ireland.

---

[200] IFUT Annual Report 1984, p. 10.
[201] IFUT Annual Report 1986, p. 23.
[202] IFUT Annual Report 1989, p. 15.

Conclusion

One of the principal aims of this study has been to highlight the importance of the dual role of the Irish Federation of University Teachers as both a professional association and a trade union. It originated as a body concerned solely with educational issues, but the recognition that the academic community needed to organise itself effectively to deal with salary negotiations brought pressure on the Federation to develop a new role in the area of industrial relations. Instances such as the dismissal of the Maynooth lecturers, the closure of Carysfort and the attempt by Trinity College to dismiss a tenured academic have all served to reinforce the need for an academic trade union. As a trade union IFUT has set up effective and successful salary negotiating machinery, and it has established its right as a trade union to represent members whose conditions of employment are under threat, thus affording greater protection to its members.

While at times it may appear that the Federation is preoccupied with salaries, pay scales and grades of lectureships, it has not lost sight of its roots as a professional association concerned with the future development of higher education in Ireland. The intensive lobbying campaign undertaken recently in response to the universities bill, and the number of amendments to it which were secured, serves to highlight IFUT's concern with educational issues. Perhaps the greatest success of the Irish Federation of University Teachers as a professional association lies in giving the academic community a greater say in government plans for higher education;

IFUT is now recognised as the body which represents academic opinion, at university level, in Ireland. This role is especially significant in view of the greater level of control which the government has exerted in the area of higher education since the 1960s.

The Federation still faces many challenges in both of its capacities. As a trade union it has to find a means of dealing with developments which threaten the security of its members' jobs, such as the increasing trend towards temporary employment. This casualisation of labour in the academic community is a trend to which the Federation is strongly opposed. In educational matters, a particularly pressing concern at the moment is to offset the detrimental impact of massification, by campaigning for increased funding for facilities to cope with larger student numbers. Resistance is also continuing to the climate of the 1990s which has sought to apply industrial criteria on productivity and cost-effectiveness to university teaching.

The membership of IFUT has shown a sustained annual growth throughout the 1990s, a recognition within the academic community of the serious challenge which these developments pose to the future of higher education, and of the need for academics to have an effective voice to represent their opinions.

IFUT - A History

Appendix 1

Chairmen and Presidents of IFUT, 1965-1998

Chairmen
- 1965-66: J.J. Morrissey (UCD)
- 1966-67: J.J. Morrissey
- 1967-68: J.J. Morrissey
- 1968-69: T. Desmond Williams (UCD)
- 1969-70: George Dawson (TCD)
- 1970-71: Seán Lavelle (UCG)
- 1971-72: Robin Dudley Edwards (UCD)

Presidents
- 1972-73: Enda McDonagh (Maynooth)
- 1973-74: Enda McDonagh
- 1974-75: Kader Asmal (TCD)
- 1975-76: Seosamh Hanly (UCD)
- 1976-77: Seosamh Hanly
- 1977-78: Patrick J. O'Flynn (UCD)
- 1978-79: Patrick J. O'Flynn
- 1979-80: John L'Estrange (UCD)
- 1980-81: Fergus Lalor (UCC)
  Bernard McCartan (TCD)
- 1981-82: Bernard McCartan
- 1982-83: Bernard McCartan
- 1983-84: Keith Warnock (UCG)
- 1984-85: Keith Warnock
- 1985-86: John Lewis (DIAS)
- 1986-87: John Lewis
- 1987-88: Garrett Barden (UCC)
- 1988-89: Garrett Barden

1989-90:   Caroline Hussey (UCD)
1990-91:   Caroline Hussey
1991-92:   Caroline Hussey
1992-93:   Anne Clune (TCD)
1993-94:   Anne Clune
1994-95:   Eugene Wall (MICL)
1995-96:   Eugene Wall
1996-97:   Eugene Wall
1997-98:   Maureen Killeavy (UCD)
1998-99:   Maureen Killeavy
1999-   :   Maureen Killeavy

Appendix 2

Secretaries of IFUT, 1965 -

Honorary Secretaries

1965-66:	David Thornley (TCD)
1966-67:	David Thornley
1967-68:	David Thornley
1968-69:	David Thornley
1969-70:	Frank Anderson (UCD)
1970-71:	Richard Conroy (RCSI)
1971-72:	Richard Conroy
1972-73:	John L'Estrange (UCD)
1973-74:	John L'Estrange
1974-75:	Patrick J. O'Flynn (UCD)
1975-76:	Anne Clissman [Clune] (TCD)
1976-77:	Patrick Collins (RCSI)
1977-78:	Caroline Hussey (UCD)
1978-79:	Caroline Hussey
1979-80:	Douglas McLernon (TCD)
1980-81:	Seán Tobin (UCG)
1981-82:	George Delafield (UCC)
1982-83:	George Delafield
1983-84:	Ferdinand Von Prondzynski (TCD)
1984-85:	Noreen Kearney (TCD)

General Secretaries*

1975-80:	Kieran Mulvey
1980- :	Daltún Ó Ceallaigh

* Originally styled Executive Secretary

Appendix 3

Original rules of IFUT adopted at its first annual general meeting, 26 March 1966

1. The name of the association shall be the Irish Federation of University Teachers.

2. The objects of the Federation shall be the advancement of higher education and research, the exchange of information in relation to common academic problems amongst its members, the promotion of a community of interest among them, and the safeguarding of their common interests.

3. Membership of the Federation shall be open to:
(i) all full-time and permanent part-time members of the academic staff of a University or University College or recognised College of a University in Ireland
(ii) in the case of any other institution of higher learning in Ireland recognised by the Council of the Federation such as those members of the academic staff who are in the opinion of the Council engaged wholly or mainly in work of university status.

4. The year shall run from 1 October to 30 September.

5. Persons may become members of the Federation either by the payment of an individual subscription, to be agreed annually by the Annual General Meeting, to the Treasurer of the Federation, or through their membership of an academic staff association which applies and is accepted by the Council for affiliation to the Federation. In the latter case, the an-

nual subscription of the affiliated body will be due in advance, on the last day of the previous year (i.e. 30 September), the amount of this subscription being a sum equal to one half of the current subscription for individual membership of the Federation, multiplied by the number of members of the affiliated body on that date (i.e. 30 September).

6. The Federation shall hold at least one general meeting every year. An extraordinary general meeting may be called on requisition signed by not less than forty members or at the written request of any two affiliated associations or electoral constituencies. A meeting thus requisitioned shall be called within thirty days of the request being received by the Chairman or Secretary, upon notice sent at least ten days before the date of the meeting. The quorum at general meetings shall be thirty and one representative of each of at least three affiliated associations or electoral constituencies must be present. The rules of the Federation may be amended only at a general meeting. A two-thirds majority of the members present shall be required in order to carry a motion proposing an alteration in the rules.

7. In the intervals between general meetings the business of the Federation shall be conducted by a Council elected in the following manner: The members of the staff at any University; University College; recognised College, or an Institution recognised under the Rule 3 above, who are paid-up members of the Federation, either by individual or corporate subscription, shall form an electoral constituency for the purpose of choosing representatives upon the Council. In

any University, University College, recognised College or Institution in which there exists a staff association which is affiliated to the Irish Federation of University Teachers, such staff associations shall nominate representatives to the Council; where no such affiliated staff association exists, an electoral college shall be constituted for the purpose. Subject to the approval of the Council such electoral college may adopt such electoral procedures as it finds suitable to its circumstances. Representatives from each electoral constituency or affiliated staff association shall be elected or nominated to the Council upon the following ration of membership on the previous 30 September.

Number of members of electoral constituency or affiliated staff association	Number of representatives on Council
20	1
21-40	2
41-60	3
61-80	4
81-100	5
101-130	6
131-160	7
161-200	8

plus one further representative for every additional fifty members or part thereof. In addition the Council may co-opt not more than three additional members in each year from among the members of the Federation. The quorum at a Council meeting shall be ten.

8. The officers of the Federation shall be a Chairman, Deputy Chairman, Secretary, and Treasurer, or be elected by the Council each year from among its elected, nominated, or co-opted members, at the first Council meeting after the conclusion of the elections or nominations to the Council. No member may serve on the Council for more than four consecutive years. The Council shall meet at least three times per year, of which meetings at least one shall be held outside Dublin. It may appoint committees, which shall be responsible to the Council, to work upon special projects which fall within the objects of the Federation.

9. The funds of the Federation shall be employed for any purpose which, in the opinion of the Council, furthers the objects of the Council. An auditor shall be appointed annually by the Annual General Meeting and an audited financial statement shall be presented by the Treasurer to the Annual General Meeting.

10. In the interpretation of these rules the decision of the Council shall be final, subject to appeal to a general meeting, when such decisions may be reversed by a two-thirds majority of the members present.

Appendix 4

IFUT Member institutions

Church of Ireland College of Education
Cork Dental Hospital
Dublin Dental Hospital
Dublin Institute for Advanced Studies
Froebel College of Education
Health Research Board
Irish School of Ecumenics
Mary Immaculate College, Limerick
Mater Dei Institute of Education
Milltown Institute of Theology and Philosophy
National University of Ireland, Maynooth
Royal College of Surgeons in Ireland
Royal Irish Academy
St. Catherine's College of Home Economics, Sion Hill
St. Patrick's College, Drumcondra
Trinity College Dublin
University College Cork - National University of Ireland, Cork
University College Dublin - National University of Ireland, Dublin
National University of Ireland, Galway

Sources and Bibliography

IFUT, 11 Merrion Square, Dublin 2
IFUT files
  Minutes of Annual General Meetings and Annual Delegate Conferences
  Minutes of Council and Executive meetings
  Files on unionisation
  Files on IAUPL
  Press statements

University College Dublin Archives Department
Robin Dudley Edwards papers

Newspapers
The Irish Times

IFUT Publications
Contemporary Developments in University Education [I], UCD ASA, November 1963; *II*, November 1964; *III*, November 1965; *IV* November 1966; *V* November 1967; *VI* February 1971; *VII* February 1972
Report of the Council, April 1967
The Proposed Merger with TCD, UCD ASA, May 1967
The Proposed University of Dublin, 22 September 1967
University Co-operation in Dublin, 2 November 1968
Theology in the University, 1969
Catholics and Trinity College, January 1970
Report on Academic-Administrative Structure, UCD ASA, October 1972

University Education in Ireland - Report from the Council, 1974
University Financing in Ireland, March 1976
Report on University Government, October 1976
Innovation and Improvement in Teaching and Learning in Higher Education, Joachim Beug (ed.), June, 1977
University Entrance Requirements and their Effect on Second Level Curricula, John Coolahan (ed.), 1979
Third-level Education in Modern Irish Society - Papers of IFUT Conference, special edition of *Social Studies*, Irish Journal of Sociology, Summer 1983
Submissions to the Curriculum & Examinations Board, 1986/87
OECD Review of Irish Education, 1986/87
Submission to the National Board for Science and Technology on 'Barriers to Research and Consultancy in the Higher Education Sector', IFUT, 1986/87
Education Action Programme - IFUT Response, 1984
A Technological University?, 1987
The Place of Higher Education in Modern Society, 1994
Academics Don't Have Babies!, Anne Byrne & Nuala Keher Dillon, February 1996
The Origins and Development of ICUTO 1982-96, Daltún Ó Ceallaigh, August 1996
   ICUTO 1982-1996 - Documents, August 1996
   The Origins etc. - Supplement 1996-98, March 1999
Future of the Universities?, August 1996
The Universities Bill 1996 - Proposals for Amendment, 1996
The Universities Act, 1997 - IFUT Triumphs, 1997

IFUT Rules, June 1998
IFUT Annual Reports
IFUT News, 1973-
Equality News

Interviews

Jim Dooge, 9 February 1999
Enda McDonagh, 22 February 1999
Kieran Mulvey, 10 February 1999
Daltún Ó Ceallaigh, 7 December 1998
Patrick J. O'Flynn, 16 December 1998
Val Rice, 25 February 1999

Official Publications

Commission on Higher Education, *Report of the Commission on Higher Education, 1960-1967.* Dublin: Stationery Office, 1967

Commission on Higher Education, *Summary of the Report of the Commission on Higher Education.* Dublin, Stationery Office, 1967

Labour Court, *Recommendation No. 3018: University Colleges Cork, Dublin & Galway and Trinity College, Dublin - Applications of Anomaly Award to Full-Time Academic and Administrative Staffs,* 5 July 1973

Secondary Sources

Coolahan, John. *Irish Education: its History and Structure.* Dublin: Institute of Public Administration, 1981
The ASTI and Post-primary Education in Ireland. Dublin: ASTI, 1984

Corish, Patrick J. *Maynooth College, 1795-1995*. Dublin: Gill & Macmillan, 1995

FitzGerald, Garrett. *All in a Life: an autobiography*. Dublin: Gill & Macmillan, 1991

Hussey, Gemma. *At the Cutting Edge: cabinet diaries, 1982-1987*. Dublin: Gill & Macmillan, 1990